Jeremy Jingwei

HUNDREDS OF PERSPECTIVES

Your favourite Bible stories

in a different and fun perspective

VOLUME TWO

H2H Books Canada

2011

Published by H2H Books Canada

Library and Archives Canada Cataloguing in Publication

Jingwei, Jeremy, 1999-
Hundreds of perspectives : your favorite Bible stories
in a different and fun perspective, vol. 2.

ISBN 978-0-9876711-5-8

1. Bible stories, English--Juvenile literature. I. Title.

BS551.3.J56 2011   j220.9'505   C2011-904719-5

Printed in the United States of America

Other Titles by Jeremy Jingwei

Table of Contents

Genesis

part one

Babel, the Tower
God's View

I watched as Noah, my faithful servant, and his sons had children, and watched them multiply throughout the earth. I saw that they all spoke one language. They all gathered together in the large plains of Babylonia. It seems like there were some skilled men who knew how to build in the bunch of them.

"This is how to build with clay." One said, as he taught another one how to make a brick.

"The tower that we're going to build, is going to be greater, and bigger than any other tower ever made." They said to each other. "We will make ourselves known throughout the earth!"

"It will reach the heavens, so that we don't have to rely on God to bring us there!" One asked.

"Yes, of course. Then we will be famous throughout the world for our cleverness." Another one added.

"We will soon rule the world and everybody shall bow down to us! We will be more powerful and stronger than anyone!" They said with pride. I laughed as they said that.

"I wonder how they will rule this world. Only I can rule this world. I created it, it is rightfully mine." I declared as the heavens shook.

"Even God will fear us, because we will make a tower up to heaven." They said as they worked. How could they think that?

"How will I fear such a small group of humans?" I asked an angel right beside me.

"These foolish men are not thinking properly. I don't know how they think they can overpower you; the God of all creation and the God. You should be feared by all!" The angel replied.

"We shall make war with all the other tribes, capture them and show them how powerful we are." The men said to each other, as they built a fortress around the tower that was being built, as well as a city around the tower.

"Yeah, and how powerful are you exactly?" An angel joked. We all laughed, and heaven shook from our laughter.

"I don't think they're even close to powerful compared to you." Another angel added.

"We've got seven layers already!" Somebody announced to the rest of the men who were working. They built it in a pyramid shape.

"What are you going to do?" An angel asked, "The tower is approaching the sky."

"I will babble their languages." I said, thinking of the plan, "They can never build something when they all speak different languages." Everybody chuckled. They all laughed. I gave the people a warning before I babbled their languages.

"From this hour on," I said, "You all will speak different languages." "Qui est vous?" One asked in French.

"Who are you?" Said another in English. We all laughed as all of the people were mixed up. The tower didn't get finished, so I destroyed it and all the people scattered and they were torn apart and couldn't speak to one other until hundreds of years later.

Genesis 9: 1-9

The City of Haran
Abram's View

"Abram!" My father shouted. I was scared I was in big trouble. Most of the time, he gets angry at us, and then he starts yelling like crazy and asks us to go to him, and there he would spank us. He is mean sometimes when he is happy, but most of time he nice. He gives us treats like getting to eat some figs he found on our trees. I love it when he's happy and nice. That's why my brother, Haran (there's also a town nearby our city, Ur called Haran) my other brother, Nahor and I always do our best to keep him happy. He doesn't frown when we try to make him happy like when we tell him tell jokes or do what he says.

"Yes, father?" I replied.

"Come here right now!" He said, sternly.

"Yes." I said as I walked over. As I walked into my father's tent I saw that the milk pail had spilt. I knew it was Haran. He liked playing pranks on my father. My father always thinks it's me, because I'm the clumsy one in the family. I wonder how it feels to be always doing everything good, and never doing anything wrong.

"Who did this?" Father asked me.

"I didn't." I said, "I think it was Haran, because he likes doing pranks on you, and because he had a big argument with me, so I think he would do this just so I could get in trouble." I told Father. He nodded. He didn't even get mad at me.

"You could leave for a little and then when I ask you to come back in, you have to come back in, okay?" Father asked me.

"Okay." I said. I went over, back to my tent. It wasn't as small as Nahor's, but it was still considered pretty small. I wonder where Mom and Father got their tents. Their tents are humongous.

Nahor, my other brother, doesn't get involved in almost anything. All he does is tend the animals, do his chores and gives our Father a hug, and goes to eat, and after our meal, he goes to bed. He sometimes does other stuff, like help with cooking or stuff, but usually he only does his own stuff. He's not very involved with other people. I wonder why he doesn't talk with a lot of people. He always tries to stop Haran and I from arguing, but it's no use if you try to stop me and Haran. All we do is go into a corner and start arguing.

"What are you doing, Haran or Abram?" He asks as we are trying to get each other into trouble. He's always trying to be the best out of all of us. He's always helping people, he's always thinking that he's the best and all that. I wonder why he's always thinking that he's the best. He never gets anything. It's kind of weird. Haran and I are always getting treats while Nahor is trying to be good, and never gets anything. Sometimes, he gets so sulky that he just stays in his tent and fasts.

"Abram, you can come back in!" Father shouted. I quickly went in. There, I saw, Father, Haran and Nahor.

"Haran blamed Nahor for doing this, and Nahor blamed you." Father said. "I can trust Haran, the most, for being the eldest, and Nahor, for being the second eldest. Although I have a feeling it was Haran, I know that Nahor is the one to blame, for I can see that his hands and face still have milk stains. I looked at Haran. It was true. He did have dabs of milk on his mouth.

Nahor suddenly looked embarrassed. We all knew it was him. It was him playing the pranks all along. It wasn't Haran doing it. I shouldn't have blamed Haran all along. So, basically, we blamed each other for doing it, not knowing that the loner did the thing.

"Nahor, you shall be punished by tending to the sheep for Abram and Haran." Father said. Haran and I both gasped. Nobody ever wanted to tend to the sheep because it was the worst thing Father could tell us to do. I wonder how Nahor will survive this horrible punishment.

"Haran and Abram, you may come with me to go hunt." He said. Haran and I rejoiced. All of us wanted to go hunting with Father, so he could show us how to catch animals for food. Afterwards, Mother would go and prepare a delicious meal for us.

"Nahor, hurry up!" Father shouted. Nahor gave the tent one last glance, then, he ran off to go tend the sheep.

"Hahaha!" Haran and I laughed together as we sat in Father's tent. Father looked stern at us for a while, then we went to go and watch him hunt.

Nahor was watching in the distance. He wasn't even paying attention to working. I wonder why. He must be feeling lonely but it is his consequence for doing that all along.

Nahor tends to the sheep without word. Father thinks he might be lonely and so Haran and I have to tend the sheep with him for a part of the time.

As we sat down for our meal which Father had caught for us, he told us that we are going to Haran. Haran seems a little excited but I think I will miss living in Ur.

"Abram! Fix your tent!" Father shouted. I hurried up. I got all my things, helped my father get into the cart with all our stuff and then, we slowly started on our way to Haran.

About halfway there, Haran was already getting impatient. "Father, are we there yet?" Haran asked. You could tell he was excited by the way he was walking quickly.

"Just wait a little longer." Father said. After waiting for what seemed a day, we started seeing the magnificent buildings, the high trees and the fortressed wall.

"How grand!" Haran exclaimed.

"Yes, it is." Father sighed as we entered our new home. It wasn't just a tent anymore. Made with clay, it was well put together. Nahor seemed to be lost within the walls. Haran could barely hold himself together.

"We're going to be living here." Father said. We all liked the place. There was a marketplace, a grand tower, with all these strong soldiers in it and there was the wall. There were other buildings too. Father dragged us all around the city.

"Haran! Hurry up!" We all shouted as we got Haran to come along. He really liked the city. That was why he was staring at everything.

We lived there for about twenty five years until I left. The city is now in ruins and we moved into tents once more. Ah! How I wish we could once more live in the comfort of the clay homes in Haran. But I am a grown man now and realize that the city may look beautiful on the outside, but it may never last forever.

Genesis 11: 31- 32

Sodom and Gomorrah
Interview

Abraham was a great man in the history of mankind. He followed the Lord faithfully. He is going to tell us about Sodom and Gomorrah.

Q: Abraham, when did the destruction of Sodom and Gomorrah happen?

A: It was about right after we settled in Caanan

Q: Sorry to be nosy, but where is Caanan?

A: Caanan is a country off the Mediterranean Sea. It was fertile.

Q: Where is Caanan, now in modern days?

A: Caanan is now where Israel, Jordan and Lebanon are today.

Q: Why do you think that God sent the harsh punishment to the people of Sodom and Gomorrah?

A: I think that he did it because they were evil in his eyes.

Q: Give me an example of being evil in God's eyes.

A: An example might be lying, murdering, being wicked, and saying rude things.

Q: What did you think when you say Lot's wife get swallowed up by the storm and turned into a pillar of salt?

A: I actually didn't see it. The Lord told us not to look behind. So, if I looked at Lot's wife, I would've become salt too.

Q: Do you think that there should've been some people rescued from there?"

A: Of course not. If it is God's will, it should not be rejected.

Q: Are you sorrowful that a lot of your friends there were killed by God?

A: I was a little saddened. However I knew that it was God's will after all, so, I guess that I shouldn't be too sorrowful.

Q: What did the storm look like?

A: It looked like a whirlwind, and then I heard a loud roaring sound that almost burst my eardrums

Q: What was the sky like when you were running?

A: The sky was pouring with rain, and it was covered with green clouds.

Q: What was the ground like when the storm was raging?

A: The ground was shaking like an earthquake.

Q: Okay. If you had to rebuild Sodom and Gomorrah, how many people would you bring with you?

A: I would only bring a few families. One of the main reasons of Sodom and Gomorrah were both crowded with wicked men was that they simply had too many people living in the cities.

Q: What did the angels that Lot saw look like?

A: Well, first of all, they both had clothing that were shining like lightning.

Q: Okay, let's keep on going. What did you think when you heard cries of help from Sodom and Gomorrah?

A: Well, at first, I kind of felt sorry for them. But, I know that they deserve the punishment.

Q: How did you feel, when the storm took a lot of your wealth and riches?

A: Well, I knew that having a lot of wealth may make a human feel good, but when you put it above God, it becomes your downfall. I guess that God sensed that in me, so I guess it was for my own good.

Q: What did you think was amazing about that day?

A: I think that God's ability to destroy Sodom and Gomorrah and save Lot and my family.

Q: What do you think about this fertile land that God gave your descendants, which was located on the ruins of Sodom and Gomorrah?

A: It is a blessing that God has given my descendants this land, since it is fertile, and filled with water, and everything suitably fits.

Q: This is my last question, okay?

A: Okay.

Q: Why did you settle here in Caanan, again, after Sodom and Gomorrah were destroyed?

A: Well, I just felt better when I knew that I was safe there.

Q: Thank you, Abraham, for your time.

A: No problem, thank you.

Genesis 13-19

100 Years
Sarah's View

"The Lord says that you will have a child in one month." An angel had appeared to me. Amusingly, I laughed. I was already 90 years old – how could I have a baby?

"How can I have a baby? Especially someone as old as me?" I chuckled.

"Do not doubt the Lord's words for he is the Lord Almighty." The angel said to me. She went away and I went to see my husband.

"Abraham, the angel of God says that I will have a baby." I said to him, who was about ten years older than I.

"Do not doubt the Lord's words for everything he says, he will do. He has shown us this by taking care of us for so long. Has he ever forsaken us?" Abraham said to me. He was much wiser than me, and I respected what he said..

"But, I still think that it is a joke!" I said. "I can't have a baby. I'm already 90 years old."

"It is not impossible." Abraham told me. "Nothing is impossible for the Lord, the one and only high God, who is glorified throughout the earth."

"But it seems impossible." I said, "I don't think anybody's done it before."

"I'm sure that God, will help you." Abraham told me.

"Yes, I'm sure that God will take care of me." I said, as I went back outside to tend his sheep and camels. Something told me to go and ask God for help.

"God, if you are so powerful, will you please help me with this child? And please dearly forgive me for laughing at your angel. It seemed funny at that time." I prayed whole-heartedly.

"Your sins are forgiven, Sarah." The Lord answered me in a faint whisper. "Your baby will have no trouble."

"Thank you Lord." I prayed again.

"Mistress Sarah, it's time for dinner." One of my maidservants said, as I got up, and I went to go eat.

"Thank you Lord, for this day, thank you Lord for this food, Amen." Abraham prayed as we quietly ate and had our food. I was starving today since I didn't eat anything since the break of dawn. I didn't want to eat lunch. I just wanted to stay in my room, and there, I saw the angels.

"Abraham, did you know that our baby is coming in 1 month?" I told him.

"Yes, I knew that because the Lord has already provided me with a dream." He said,

Thank Goodness that I didn't have to get shouted at! I thought

"What's this?" I asked as I saw a small piece of cloth that had fallen on the ground.

You Are Blessed with A Child. He Shall One Day, be Great, and his descendants will be a powerful nation

"Abraham! Quick, look at this!" I shouted and he immediately came over. He's usually doesn't hang around my tent, but ever since the angels came, he's been here more frequently.

"This must be a note from the Lord!" Abraham said. I quickly fell down on the ground in prayer and amazement.

"Thank you Lord, for giving us strength. Thank you for bringing us here. Thank you for showing us all these signs! Please help us and give us strength during these hardships. Thank you. Amen." Abraham and I prayed.

The next month went by faster than ever. Abraham and all of the other maids and servants were excited for the child. I could almost feel him inside of me, waiting to jump out.

"It's the last day of the month already!" I said, thinking. On the last day of the last month, the Lord sent angels to tell me that that day, I would have baby.

"Abraham, look at him!" I said. It was the first baby that I've ever had, and he looked so cute.

"What shall we name him?" I asked.

"The Lord told me in a dream that we should name him Isaac," Abraham said.

"I like the name Isaac." I said, thoughtfully. Isaac is a nice name. I wouldn't have thought of it personally, but now, that it comes to my mind, I think it will fit.

"Yes, we will name him Isaac." I said.

"Hello," A crowd shouted. Isaac and I both looked around. There was a whole crowd of our servants. They came and gave gifts of silver and gold.

"We want to thanks all of you, for your service, and today, for a special occasion, we will hold a feast for everyone to enjoy!" Abraham exclaimed as everyone started chattering about the feast.

"Thank you Lord, for this child, for I've been waiting for one for 100 years." Abraham thanked the Lord. I too, was happy, and honoured to be the mother of this boy! *Thank you Lord!* I said as I got down and sat for the feast with Isaac on my leg, sitting happily.

Genesis 17 and 21

The Lord Provides
Isaac's View

"He's now three years old." Mother proudly said to Father.

"Yes, I shall take him out on a trip today." Father said. He looked sorrowful at me.

"Come on, you two." Father pointed to two of our servants. Father and I rode on a donkey, while the servants walked on ground beside us.

"What's that?" I asked Father. It looked like a big mound of dirt, with rocks piled on it, and there was grass on it, there were also a few wild animals roaming here and there.

"That's a mountain." Father said.

"Are we going to go on it?" I asked.

"Yes." Father answered, bluntly, trying to end the conversation.

"Stay here on the donkey." He said pointing to the servants. "My boy and I will be back soon."

Then, Father went do a nearby place, where he found some wood.

"What's that for?" I asked, pointing to the wood.

"It's for a fire." Father said.

"Why would we need a fire?" I asked. Father said we were coming up here just for a little walk which was why I was confused.

"I'm going to build an altar to sacrifice things to God." Father answered.

"What's an altar?" I asked. Father's using really large words and I don't know what they mean. I hope that I'll learn what everything means before I grow older.

"It something that you give sacrifices to God." Father answered.

"What type of sacrifices?" I asked.

"Normally, I would put a lamb on it." Father said.

"What's a lamb?" I asked confused. Dad's used another word that I don't know the meaning.

"A lamb is a young sheep." Father answered.

"Young sheep from the herd?" I asked.

"Yes, dear Isaac." Father answered.

"Well, what are you waiting for, let's go sacrifice a lamb." I said.

"We don't have a fire yet." Father said.

"Are you going to build one?" I asked him.

"Yes, just, I have to get some hot burning coals." Father said, as he pulled out little black rocks and put them on the wood.

"How long is it going to take?" I asked him.

"A little longer, son." Dad answered, trying to mask the sadness in his eyes.

I was impatient for this fire to be made. We didn't even bring a lamb; I don't know what type of sacrifices father was making his God.

"Is the fire ready now?" I asked.

"Yes." Father said. He looked like he was going to cry.

Maybe, he doesn't want to sacrifice to lamb. It might be too painful.

"Father," I said pleadingly. "We have the fire ready from the wood and coals, and also an altar for the sacrifice, but where is the goat that we need to sacrifice for the offering?" I asked.

"The Lord always provides what we need." Father said, as he took ropes, and suddenly, he tied my hands together and my feet together.

"Father, get rid of these things!" I shouted as I tried to get out of them, but they were too tight.

"Why are you doing this to me?" I asked Father, he didn't respond. Then, he put me on the altar and tied me on to it.

"Are you going to sacrifice me?" I asked, terrified. Now, my own Father was going to kill me!

"Yes."

"Why Father? Aren't I your only son?" I asked.

"It is God's will." He said, sadly. I was blindfolded with Father's cloths. He pulled out something which I knew was a knife. He was going to sacrifice me.

I prepared for the pain in my stomach as the knife hit it and I closed my eyes, but nothing happened. Instead, I heard a voice.

"Abraham, Abraham," it said. "Do not touch the boy. Now that I know how great your trust is in God, you need not sacrifice your son."

"Father, who is he?" I asked. The voice sounded like none other; sweet yet confident.

"He's the Lord Almighty." Father replied, then untied me and let me free.

"Father, look, there's a lamb over the over there!" I shouted. There was a lamb, stuck in the trees.

"The Lord always provides." Father said as he went to catch the lamb and put it on the altar. I then watched as he sacrificed the lamb in the fire.

"Because you were prepared to sacrifice your only son for my sake, I will give you as many descendants as there are stars in the sky." The Lord said.

Father took me home again as though nothing had happened. Mother was there waiting for us. I ran to her happily and Father stood there, tired, yet anxious to do the work of the Lord.

Genesis 22

The Drink for the Camels
Eliezer's View

"Eliezer!" My master Abraham shouted. I ran towards him.

"Yes, master, I am here." I reported quickly.

"I have a special task for you." My master Abraham said.

"Yes, I will gratefully do it for you, master." I said. "What is the task?"

"My task is for you to find a wife for my son, Isaac. I am getting too old to travel, but you are still young. I don't want you to find him a Caananite woman near where we live. I want you to find someone who lives in my birth land, Mesopotamia. Perhaps you could stay at Bethuel's home while you search for someone." Master Abraham explained, as I nodded. Bethuel was a relative of Abraham.

"I will gladly do the task." I said. Although I had really no idea what to do, I thought common sense. "I shall need to bring a few gold armbands, 10 camels, several vials of water, a sack of bread, gold, silver, and precious jewels." I said.

"Yes, that should be all you need." My master said.

"Then, I shall be off soon." I said. Everyone could tell that my master is growing older and older. He's also really sullen after Sarah, his wife died. I'm kind of sad too. Sarah was always nice to me, and she always gave me gifts.

"Farewell until I return!" I said, as I waved farewell to Isaac, and Abraham, both in the fields.

"Farewell," They said, as their figures grew smaller and smaller, as I advanced through the desert, in search of Bethuel, Abraham's relative. I hope that I can find someone suitable for Isaac.

It's already night, I thought, as the sun was fading away, and the stars started appearing.

"Lord, how can I find someone, when it's already been a day?" I prayed.

"I shall tell you; you will see a well tomorrow. You shall ask for a drink. If a woman asks you if your camels want a drink too, then, she'll be the one." The Lord told me.

"So if a woman asks you if your camels want a drink too, then, she'll be the one." I said again.

"Yes." The Lord replied

"Do you swear by an oath?" I asked.

"Yes, I do." The Lord replied.

It's morning already, I must get moving, and I must find the well that the Lord has told me about, I thought as I got up, saddled the camels and we kept on going.

"Here must be the well God was talking about." I said to myself as I looked around for any sign of someone who might be suitable for Isaac.

"May I please have a drink?" I asked a beautiful lady who was carrying a bucket.

She went and fetched a bucket of water for me. "Would your camels like a drink too?" She offered.

"You must be the one!" I shouted.

"What?" She asked.

"The Lord told me last night, that whoever offers me a drink and my master's camels a drink shall be the wife of Abraham's son!" I was overjoyed.

"Who is your father?" I asked.

"Bethuel is my father. Laban is my brother. My name is Rebekah" She said.

"We shall head off as soon as you can say goodbye to your family, and bring your servants and belongings." I said quickly.

"The Lord does what he says, so, I will not doubt his words." Rebekah said.

"Father, Uncle Abraham has a son, and God says that I shall be his wife." Rebekah said.

"If God says so, than carry it on." Bethuel said, "First, may she stay with us for a little?"

"Sure, but not for too long. Not over a day. Tomorrow, you shall bring your things and we shall be off to Abraham's land." I said.

"Okay, then, one day it is." Laban, Rebekah's brother said.

"It's time to go, Rebekah!' I shouted as Rebekah and her servants got on the camels and we started off back to Caanan. The harsh sun was scorching my back and everyone else looked hungry, so I started looking for some type of shade, where we could have some food, before we started again, to Caanan.

I hope that we can make it to Abraham's place, before the sun sets. If we don't, then it'll be another day. I like to make my treks short and easy, for then I can rest right after.

"It's time to go!" I said as we got on our camels and started heading into the direction of Abraham's encampment. Not after long, I saw fertile grass, and fields. I knew we were here at Abraham's.

"Who is that?" Rebekah asked, pointing to Isaac.

I smiled. "That is my master's son."

Genesis 24

Twins, Rivals, Enemies
Jacob's View

I looked at my older brother Esau go out first before I did. He had hairy red hair all over. I looked at myself, all clean with smooth black-brown hair on my head only.

As we grew up, our differences grew more distinct. Esau went hunting and he was my father's favourite son. My mother, Rebecca, loved me more than Esau and I helped her in the kitchens.

When I grew up, the firstborn sons always had the rights and privileges. Usually, if my father died, the firstborn son would get all his inheritances, which typically unfair to me. Esau got everything and I had to serve my older brother.

I wanted those privileges more than ever and I thought of a tricky plan to get them from Esau. When he was desperate, I would then take them from him.

One day, after Esau came home from hunting, he was exhausted and desperately hungry. He asked me for some stew. I knew that this was the perfect time.

"Only if you give me your firstborn rights." I said and he agreed. That was how much he valued his firstborn rights! If I had known sooner, then I would have probably had them by now!

"Just give me the stew and it'll be yours." He said as he agreed. I gave him a small bowl of stew and a piece of bread. When he finished eating, he resumed to go hunting.

When we grew up, I did something that made our rivalry even worse. My father, Isaac, his eyesight began to fail and he couldn't see. He called my brother, Esau and told him that he would bless Esau if he would go and hunt an animal for my father to eat. My mom, Rebecca, listened in as sneaky as she was. She always wanted me to have the blessing instead of Esau. So she told me to go fetch a goat so she could prepare the meat for Isaac.

"Change into Esau's clothes." She said as I pulled them over my shirts. She cut off the goat skin and placed them over my arms. Then she sent me off to my father, who was sitting in his tent.

"Hello Father." I said.

His eyesight was failing so he could not tell who I was. "Who are you?"

"I am Esau, your firstborn. Here is the meat I prepared." I offered him the meat and he looked astounded.

"How did you get it so fast?" He asked. My mother stood in the corner, helping me with what to say.

"God helped me." My father was still not convinced. I rolled my eyes. This was going to take forever. And what if Esau comes in right now? I asked myself.

"Come closer, and let me feel your arms." I held out the arms, which were the goat hairs. My father was obviously confused.

"You sound like Jacob, but yet your arms are rough like Esau's. Come closer and kiss me." I walked closer to kiss him.

"Ah, yet you smell like Esau." Then he ate the meat and he blessed me. I quickly ran out and took off his clothes and the goatskin. Rebecca smiled as I came back.

I watched as Esau came back with the meat prepared. My father became confused. My stomach felt like butterflies were flying through. I was so scared.

"Who are you?" He asked.

"I am Esau, your firstborn." Esau said.

"That couldn't be, I have already eaten." Isaac said. "Unless your brother tricked me into giving him the blessing."

Esau dropped on to the floor, crying, "I will kill Jacob, once my father dies!" He shouted to Mother. That night, Mother warned me to run even before my father dies so that I may be far away. She packed a few things with me and I set off in the middle of the night. Esau is quicker than me, so I don't know how long I will survive there or how long I survive until Esau finds me.

After a few hours of traveling, I noticed the sun falling down and the darkness emerging from its hiding spot. I would have to stay here for the night.

I looked around for a good place to sleep. I saw a stone, that didn't look too uncomfortable, so I put my head on it and fell asleep.

Then, I had a strange dream. There was a voice towering over me. "I am the God of Abraham, and your father Isaac. The land on which you sleep on will be yours. I am giving it to you, and you will have as many descendants as there are grains on the seashore. I will look after you wherever you go and will one day bring you back to this land."

The next morning, I rose up early and I poured a bit of oil, that I had in my pocket on it. I called the spot Bethel, and I promised God that if he stays and protects me, then, he will be my God.

Genesis 25 and 27

Reunion
Jacob's View

"Daddy, where are we going?" One of my sons asked.

"We're going to meet my brother Esau." I said. I was a bit afraid, but I knew the Lord was going to help me.

"You mean the one who tried to kill you before, is he going to kill us too?" They asked. Leah shushed my sons to be quieter but I told her not to.

"No, I sent slaves with presents. Even if he doesn't accept them, I will not be afraid." I told them bravely. But, I knew my brother Esau probably wouldn't accept those gifts. He is probably enraged with me at me for stealing his blessing and his birthright when I was still young. I've also heard rumours that he has 400 men with him. I wonder if he's going to attack. If he is, I should just surrender myself so that he would not kill my family.

"Your messengers are back." My eldest son, Reuben alerted as I saw the two men coming. I was afraid. They looked more scared than of happy. I looked around and I saw the two messengers there. They didn't have the presents in their hands, so I guess that Esau must have accepted them, because if he didn't, he must've seized them.

"How was the trip?" I asked the two messengers. They didn't reply to my question.

"Well, master, it wasn't as we expected." They said looking uneasy.

"What do you mean?" I asked them

"Well, we went there, and Esau looked grateful, and he didn't reply to our questions. He took the gifts and let us go." They said.

"What happened next?" I asked.

"Well, suddenly, we saw 400 men pop up out of nowhere and they started to come up behind us and encircle us, but, Esau let us go.

"That's an unusual thing." I said

"Why?" The messengers asked, confused.

"My brother Esau is known of his brutality. Why would he be nice to messengers of his brother, who stole his birthright and his blessing?" I explained to them.

"Oh." They went to the back without another word.

"Daddy, are we going to fight? I love to fight!" My son Levi said. Levi has been attacking his tent with a wooden sword that I had carved for him. He has already destroyed his tent more than once and I have no plan to get him another.

"No, Levi, I don't suspect we'll have to fight, and even if we did, you wouldn't have to because you'd be killed easily. If we do fight, it will be I who fights for it is I who needs to take the punishment for stealing things I never should took." I said. Levi burst into tears, and wailed. He got a little fussy, and so I called one of my servants to bring him out.

"Daddy, why are you so scared of your brother? He only has 400 men. We have more people than that in here." Dan, one of my smaller sons asked.

"Not all of the people here can successfully stop an attack." I said.

"What shall we do to keep some of the people safe?" Simeon, my second son said.

"I will split the people into 2 groups. If the first group is captured, then the second is safe. But, if the second is captured, the first is safe." I said.

"Here he comes!" Someone shouted. Rachel and Leah hushed the children to be silent and I walked forward. Everyone was scared. I quickly split them into two groups, and waited for Esau's arrival.

"Please forgive me!" I shouted out as I ran and a bowed down at Esau's approach.

But Esau ran to meet me and embraced me. He threw his arms around my neck and kissed my forehead. And then we, two grown men, wept there in front of the children and our wives. Then Esau looked up and saw the women and children.

"Who are these with you?" he asked.

"They are the children God has graciously given to your servant." I answered and bowed.

Then the maidservants and their children approached and bowed down. Next, Leah and her children came and bowed down. Last of all came Joseph and Rachel, and they too bowed down.

"Why did you send so many people with gifts of gold and silver?" Esau asked,
"To find favour in your eyes, my brother," I said.

"I already have plenty of gold and silver, my brother." Esau said "Keep what you have for yourself."

"Please accept it!" I pleaded. "If I have found favour in your eyes, accept this gift from me. Please accept the present that was brought to you, for God has been gracious to me and I have all I need." And because I insisted, Esau accepted it.

"I shall have to go back to Seir soon." Esau said.

"Why?" I asked.

"For I have to tend to my children and wives too," He said.

"Okay, then I'll let you be on your way." We hugged, and then, he and his men left for Seir.

"Daddy, can we get the sheep and the other animals out now?" Rueben, my eldest son asked.

"Okay." I said, "For we will celebrate that God has taken care of us, from my brother Esau, at our reunion." And that was what we did. We celebrated the reunion and how the Lord kept everyone safe.

Genesis 32-33

Out of Egypt

part two

Slavery in Egypt
An Israelite Child's View

"The Pharaoh is dead." A messenger said, with his eyes downcast. Everyone was mourning at his death, for he was right in the Lord's eyes and he treated us very kindly. Suddenly, another man stood in the crowd.

"And I shall succeed my father as the Pharaoh of Egypt." He was lean and strong, but he looked angry when he saw us Israelites. I wonder why. I hope that he isn't planning on turning us into servants or slaves. That would be horrible. We were supposed to have a rich life here.

"I have a new proclamation!" The Pharaoh said as we all looked at him. "All these people here, the Hebrews, shall become slaves. If we do not slave them, they will attack us with our enemies. We will be overwhelmed and we shall lose our empire due to these people." I gasped. We would never do something like that to where the Pharaoh used to live.

"Yes! Let us destroy these Hebrews and make them our slaves. We won't have to work in the heat of the sun. We can have our own lives in our homes, and not have to worry about constructing and building things." The Egyptian people said.

"Are you with me?" The Egyptian pharaoh asked his people. All of us Israelites were shocked, but, the Egyptians were obviously cheering. We had no choice but to become slaves. They were too loud. Their overwhelming numbers could destroy us.

"Mother, what are we going to do?' I cried.

"I don't know, but we have to put it in God's hands." Mother told me as I watched and waited.

"For my people," The pharaoh said, "I shall put you Hebrews into slavery."

"No!" A mob of us were shouting. The Egyptian Pharaoh looked at us with contempt and he asked his soldiers to send us right back home.

"You, Hebrews, our new slaves, go home!" The Egyptian soldiers shouted as they pointed their swords at our heads.

"Mother, I'm scared." I cried. Having someone behind you threatening that if you don't keep on going, they'll kill you is not a experience many people would want. But I always at least try to keep happy.

I tried to talk to my sister but Mother started trying to hush us. The Egyptians didn't seem to care. At least if we kept on walking it'd be okay to them.

I was ahead of all the Hebrews, and a few Egyptians looked cautious, but after they saw me heading for the village, the slowly relaxed and watched as we went back to our homes.

"Mother, are we really going to have to work for nothing, and then be beaten by those Egyptians?" I asked her as we all settled down glumly in our house.

"Yes, and even worse, we'll have to work from dawn to dusk, and we'll hardly get any sleep. You children will get to come home early." Mother said sleepily, as we all went to bed.

Mother and Father had their own bed in their own room, while my younger sister, my oldest sister and my older brother and I slept in the same room. My big brother and I had our own bed, while my sisters shared a bed.

"It's time to wake up!" Mother shouted. I opened my eyes. It was still dark outside. Was she crazy or what?

"Are we really supposed to wake up this early?" I asked my older brother.

"Yeah, of course, remember we're going to work today." He said. Then I remembered all the events that happened yesterday. I yawned, got up and got my clothes on. Then, I looked around for my sandals. I got them, and I hurried with the others to go outside to do slave work.

"This sure is hard work." I whispered to my brother as the slavedriver passed by.

I'd only made 3 bricks that whole entire time, and I'd already been whipped once that day. The whipping felt like a burn at first, and then, it cooled and felt better.

"Stop talking or else you'll be whipped again." He whispered when the slavedriver was gone.

"Okay then, we'll talk at home." I said.

"Can't. By the time I get home, you'll be in bed." He told me.

"What?" I asked confused

"I'm already 12. I have to do grown-up work by now." He said.

"Oh," I said.

"Children, you can go home now!" A bossy slavedriver shouted. We all obeyed and walked through the sand and we went home. My younger sister and I had a little food that Mother had prepared before breakfast and we went to bed.

"Children, we're back," Mother and Father said.

"Now that there's slavery in Egypt, we'll have no way to get out of it, unless God gives us a miracle that will convince Pharaoh. Let us pray for one."

Exodus 1

Baby Moses
Miriam's View

"Mother, hide him!" I shouted as Mother had another baby boy. Mother hid him in a basket quickly. We saw an Egyptian slave driver passing by our house.

"What have we got today?" An Egyptian slave driver entered our house.

"Nothing much, just we were having a little fun." I hurried tried to cover up because we were in odd places. We were all in odd places around the room. I was on the floor, Aaron was looking like he was about to run. And Mother was just standing there.

"Okay" He said, looking around the room sceptically. "But if I hear about you three, you'll surely be sent for extra work." The slave driver exited the house.

I sighed a huge sigh of relief, once the slave driver was out of sight. The Pharaoh told slavedrivers to throw all Hebrew baby boys in the Nile River which means my new little brother would have had to be killed. Luckily, Aaron was born a few years ago. Aaron is my little brother and he is already old enough to start to work.

Father isn't home yet from work. He works from dawn, to dusk. We children and women only work from dawn to noon. Then we get to go home. I'm lucky I'm not a boy. Once a boy's fourteen, he's considered a man and has to do full time labour out in the sands. Sometimes, women get harder jobs too.

The worst job is cooking. Mother always forces me to cook with her. I'm usually really clumsy in the kitchen, so Mother usually just gives me jobs that could use some clumsiness. Sometimes, I wish that Father was here. He used to always play games with us, until we were ordered to do extra work. Now, we have to make extra bricks, work longer.

However, whatever we do, Pharaoh seems unsatisfied with us. I wonder why. We work for him, all this time, and then, he orders to do more, ungratefully. At least he has slaves.

"Where are you going, Miriam?" Mother asked as I was walking to the exit of our small house.

"Mother, I'm going to go talk to my friend," I asked as Mother looked at me thoughtfully.

"Yes, you may, but, you may not tell about the baby." Mother answered, "If too many people know, then, Pharaoh will kill us all."

"What shall we name him, Mother?" Aaron asked Mother as I opened the door, only to find two women at the door. I looked at them but luckily, they were just our people, not those Egyptians.

"Excuse me." I said as I slipped out the door, to meet my friend, Dina. I can't wait to talk to her.

"Dina!" I shouted as I saw her, down the road. We, Israelites live in Goshen but it's only big enough to fit us Israelites so we're all packed together. We can usually find our friends easily.

"Hello, Miriam." She said. She sounded a little sad.

"Why do you sound so sad?" I asked.

"None of your business." She said.

"What's wrong? I promise I won't tell anyone, not even my parents." I pleaded.

"Okay, fine." She whispered into my ear so others couldn't hear. Tears started coming out of her eyes. "My little baby brother was killed. It would have been better if they threw him in the Nile but instead, Egyptian soldiers came into our house, when they heard my brother crying. Then, they took a sword and just killed him in one blink of the eye.

"Oh Dina!" I said as she dried off her tears. I thought of my baby brother. I wonder if he will survive, or if he will die just like Dina's brother.

"I've got a secret," I whispered to her, "Promise you won't tell anyone?"

She nodded.

"I have a new baby brother." I whispered. She looked at me with her eyes bulging with surprise.

"Really?" She whispered, "Hide him carefully."

Suddenly, Mother calling me perked my ears.

"Miriam!" Mother shouted.

"I've got to go." I said as I started running to the house.

"Yes, Mother," I said. Standing tall and straight in front of her.

"It's time for cooking supper." Mom commanded. I looked up at the sky. It was already fading. The sky was turning darker and darker.

"We shall eat lamb today, as a special celebration." Mom said.

"Can I slaughter the lamb?" Aaron asked.

"No, you may not!" Mom shouted, "Your father has already got one ready, for any special occasion."

"How are we going to cook it?" I asked, I've only eaten lamb once before in my whole entire life.

"I will teach you how." Mother said.

"Okay." I said, and we started. Mother showed me how to cook it in oil then roast it over the fire she had started with the twigs Aaron gathered from the edges of the Nile.

"Finally, we're finished." I said, as I smelled the delicious scent. It was better meat than we had these days.

"What's that basket over there for?" I asked Mother, pointing to a basket covered with tar around it.

"It's for sailing the baby." Mother confessed, I looked horrified.

"Why?"

"If we don't soon, he'll be murdered and slaughtered." Mother answered. We shall do those things tomorrow so that he can live in peace and not be murdered by these evil people." Mother said to us quietly. "Tomorrow, Miriam, your task will be to follow the basket to where it falls and make sure it doesn't get hurt. I entrust your little brother into your hands." She looked at me and I nodded to show that I understood.

"Okay."

The next day came quicker than expected. We all rushed to the Nile in the reeds so no one could see us. Then Mother placed the baby in the basket, gave him a kiss and sent him off in the water. I watched from the sides as the basket floated to all the places. He seemed to be okay.

I tracked the basket as Aaron and Mother went back home.

Suddenly, I found out where it had floated to.

We were in the Princess's bathing area.

I quickly hid behind the reeds on the side and watched as the basket floated up to the Princess.

"What is this?" She opened the basket up and there was my little brother, crying inside of the basket. She held him up and caressed him. "His name shall be Moses, for he was found by the river and he shall be kept in the Royal Palace." That was exciting! My baby brother was going to be a prince!

I scrambled out of the reeds and walked towards the princess.

"Shall I find a Hebrew slave to take care and wean him?" I asked. She seemed surprised to see me at first, but then she smiled.

"Yes, yes, go and bring him back when he is ready." She said. I took my baby brother in my hand and set off to go find my mother.

Exodus 2

The Burning Bush
A Sheep's View

"Moses, do you want to be a shepherd for me?" I heard as I looked around. I grazed into the grass. Before, we had a shepherdess, and now, we have a shepherd.

I would've wanted to have a shepherd, because they offer more protection for us. At least that's what I think. I can't wait to have a shepherd. There's some proof that shepherds give more protection.

My old shepherdess, Zipporah, let my sister get eaten by a bear. It was a sad loss. There was blood everywhere and she was completely ripped apart.

"Sure," Moses said. "I'd be glad to be your shepherd."

"Why, thank you Moses that relieves the duties of my daughters. They have been complaining about it forever." Jethro, our master said. Jethro is kind. He always gives us more than enough food. He lets us graze in his special pastures and he hardly ever uses us as meat. He often shears off our wool every once in a while, which can be refreshing.

I thought for a second.

Moses seems more than kind. He seems like he doesn't want to hurt us. But, he also looks like he is kind of scared. I hope it's not anything bad. If it is, then I'm scared. Us sheep never like it when our shepherd or shepherdess is scared. It might mean anything from a lion to a bear.

"Moses!" Jethro shouted the next day. I was shivering from the cold from last night. I wonder how Moses wakes up so late. Everyone or thing wakes up at early in the morning. Now it's almost mid-day.

"Yes, Jethro." He said as he got up, out of bed and grabbed his staff. Then he came out.

"He's real nice." All the sheep were saying. He spends all his time patting us, and giving us names. I didn't get close enough to get a name, but I got to listen to some of the silly names that he called a few of my friends.

"How was your first day, Moses?" I heard Jethro ask Moses. If I got a name, I'd probably be called long ear or something like that. I've got super long ears. Some sheep teased me about it when I was still young, but now, I prove to have better hearing than all of them. They now know better than to talk about me behind my back.

"My first day went well," Moses said as he went into his tent. I've really wanted to go in that tent ever since I was a little lamb. Everyone here in our flock wants to go there. Very few have. A few went in there because they snuck in, when nobody was there. I wonder why I didn't go in there. I probably wasn't even brave enough back then. I wasn't good at anything back then.

My mother used to tell me that one day I would grow to be a great sheep. I wonder if I'm a great sheep already.

Mother died last year, when a bear stole her from the Shepherdess. I never saw her ever again. It was very heartbreaking, as I had always grown up with my mother. Father had died right after my birth. He was somehow killed when something hit him in the head. I wonder how hard it was. I hope that it didn't hurt too much. I don't want to die such a painful death like my parents did. My only remaining family member is my Brother. He treats me pretty well but he maybe participates in a prank once in a while, but he's nicer than most other Brothers.

Last night, a wolf came and attacked our pen. Luckily, the gate was latched, and the walls were thorny, so the wolf had no chance of getting in. I wonder how anything could make it past those walls.

Moses has come out. I'm kind of bored right now. I might as just wander off just for a little bit. Moses will always find me no matter what. I'll leave my prints into the sand.

There is a shiny light in a cave! I might as well go explore it. Moses should know I'm here.

Moses has come to the rescue. Inside, what was shiny was a burning bush. It was more than just a plain old fire, it was blue.

"Moses, Moses, you are standing on the ground of the Lord, almighty, so take off your sandals." I heard a voice say. I was scared to death. Moses took off his sandals and he bent down.

"You shall go back to Egypt." The Voice said. I never knew Moses was from Egypt!

"But, the Pharaoh, he's after me!" Moses complained. He added a few other excuses, but God answered them all.

"Tell Jethro that you shall leave in a day." Was the last words the bush said. Then, I followed Moses back to the flock and there, I sat solemnly. It would be Moses' last day with us.

"Bye Moses!" We all said as he left for Egypt. I wonder if he would come back to tend us once more.

Exodus 3

The Spies of Israel
Rahab's View

"What are you two doing here?" I asked two Israelites who were under the wall.

"We want to spy in Jericho." They said.

"Why should I let you two in, if you're going to destroy my city?" I questioned.

"If we destroy Jericho, we will spare your family." The spies pleaded. They sounded pretty convincing. I just know that Jericho will fall.

"Agreed." I said. I hung a rope from the window, and I let them up.

"You know that Jericho is melting with fear from you Israelites. The King has ordered that twice the number of guards that he usually puts on the wall should be on the wall at all times. It's kind of crazy." I explained.

My home was in the wall. Suddenly, two men knocked on my door. I quickly hid the spies, in flax, and I opened the door. Two tall men came in.

"The King says that he would like you to reveal the Israelite Spies in your house, when he comes in."

I buried them deeper in the flax, so you couldn't see them, and when the King came, I had to lie to keep them safe.

"Where did the spies go?" He asked, "If they're in here, then bring them to me, so I can execute them. If I don't, the Israelites will have full information."

"I don't know where they went." I lied. "I think they went out the gate at dusk when it closes. Maybe if you bring your army out right now, you could catch up."

"Alright," the soldier said. "Men, out the gates!" The armies started pouring out the gates. When the last one was out, I quickly turned to the spies.

"You two should hide in the valleys for three days, watching our activity, and then you can go." I said. I knew that the valley was the safest place, because it was hidden. The troops wouldn't necessarily look there for spies.

"Thank you so much." They thanked, "On the day Jericho is conquered, tie a red ribbon on your windowsill, and gather your whole family in it. When the walls fall down, your family will be safe. Unless, somebody of your family goes out on the road, at the time the walls fall down. Then, their bloodshed will be on their own heads." They assured me.

"But, there is one more thing," They said, "If you tell this to any one of these people of Jericho, not including your family, the oath will be broken and you will not be saved from the wall falling down." I would do whatever the Lord told me to do if it included saving my family from this.

I put the rope down, and they climbed down, and then, they ran into the valley. I looked to see if they were there every day, and they were.

The King, came back, and he was depressed after the false pursuit. He thought that the spies had already ran away with the information. Fortunately, for the spies, he didn't know they were still in the region.

"Close the gates, nobody shall come out or come in!" The King ordered. He was tense after he learned of the Israelite attack the was coming. In the truth, he was melting with fear, and he just wanted to look tough. He had all his soldiers stand guard on the wall, with spears and arrows, if the Israelites came.

"Rahab, have you not seen the Israelites march in and out?" The King shouted. He was quite angry.

"No, my king since they dressed like all of us."

"Very well." He cleared his throat and began to speak but then I jumped in before he could speak.

"King, what shall we do, if the Israelites storm our city?" I asked the king.

"We shall abandon Jericho and go somewhere else." The King answered. Suddenly, with a loud roar I heard many footsteps.

"The Israelites are coming!" Everybody was shouting.

"What are they doing?" The guards asked. I watched as some guards started laughing, which was strange. The Israelites marched around the wall once, and left. They didn't even attack!

The same thing happened for the next 5 days.

"Rahab dear, are you sure this will save us." I assured her that the Lord God Almighty will save us from them and that they would keep their word.

"The Israelites are coming again!" Everybody shouted. They prepared to laugh as the Israelites marched around the wall. This time, they walked around not only one time, but seven times. I quickly gathered my family, and tied a scarlet ribbon on to my windowsill. After the seventh march, the Israelites made a lot of noise. Then, there was a giant shudder, and the walls trembled. It was amazing! The stone walls of Jericho were trembling without even being attacked.

BOOM! The walls went. All of the walls fell, except for my part. All the rest of the people who were inside Jericho died. I watched a few close friends die. I now know that it was a smart idea to help the Israelites. If I hadn't done it, my family wouldn't have survived the seven day march.

"Thank you!" I said to all the Israelites. Their God spared me from a death that would've been horrible. Also, if it weren't for Israel's God, my family wouldn't have survived either. There were only a few survivors of Jericho. My family and I were the only survivors.

"We will have to thank you," Joshua, the leader of the Israelites said. "If it weren't for you, our spying mission of Jericho would've failed.

All the Israelites went up to me and thanked me. I wonder why. I think I'm the one who has to thank them.

"Thank you," The two spies of Israel said, very gratefully.

"You're welcome." I said. I smiled. More and more people crowded around me. Soon, the whole crowd was done. It was about 600, 000, people, so it took almost the whole day.

"We shall head on to the city of Ai next!" Joshua announced. All the people packed up, and we moved to another campsite. I bid them farewell and luck towards their next city. May the Lord bless them.

Joshua 2 and 6

Judges

part three

The Israelites Clear out the Canaanites
A Soldier's View

"Today, the Lord has told us to clear out the Canaanites!" Our commander was shouting as we all went out towards the main square, all in attention. I wonder how we are going to do it, because all of the Canaanites together could overrun us, even in one battle. They had the latest technology, iron chariots, while all we have are javelins and spears.

"Who will join me in this battle?" The commander shouted as a line of soldiers formed. I knew that the Lord our God, would be with us and he would clearly help us in this battle against the Canaanites. I stepped into the line, and behind me a few other soldiers came in. We all marched towards an uncertain place that only our commander knew, and there, we saw our brothers, the Simeonites, camped.

"Will you go down with us, to fight for our land? We will help you fight for yours!" Our commander asked as the Simeonites all came into our line and they started marching towards our lands up north. We attacked Adoni-Bezek, which means Lord of Lightning, King of the City of Bezek.

"Charge!" Our commander shouted as we all grasped our weapons and thought of the wave of 10, 000 men who were stationed in this city. I tried not to think about death, but in the battle, there is always death for both sides.

"What's going on?" I heard Adoni-Bezek shout as he saw all his men and chariots being destroyed by javelins and spears, which were usually pretty useless in battle.

I had three men attack me at once, but, I took my javelin, and I spun around, killed all three with the tip, and I kept on running. I saw a few of my friends on the ground, but I knew that I couldn't help them now; I would have to help them after the battle.

The heat of the battle is almost unbearable I thought as I made my way into the outskirts of Bezek. The Lord our God had struck terror in the Canaanites' eyes and they were all waiting inside the city, looking terrified.

"Run!" I heard Adoni-Bezek, King of Bezek, shout as he saw that we had made our way into the city. He was so frightened that he got into a chariot and rode as fast as he could, to Jerusalem, to try to get help from his allies, the Jebusites.

"Charge!" Shouted our commander once again, and we ran as fast as we can. We threw javelins at the people in front of us, and their casualties piled up. We had no casualties. It was an uncertain battle, because they might turn back at any time and face us.

"Get Adoni-Bezek," Our commander shouted, as he saw we were nearing Jerusalem. We all picked up our weapons, and made a hailstorm at his chariot. A few broke his wheels, and then, one hit the horse. The chariot tumbled, and we pulled Adoni-Bezek out and we used his own sword and cut off his toes and his thumbs. He then muttered a few words only a few of us could hear.

"There were 70 kings under my tables with their thumbs and toes cut off, feeding on scraps, and now, I have mine cut off." He muttered, as we looked at him in a medical inspection. He was almost perfectly healthy, except for an infected cut that was swelling on his side.

"We shall lay siege on Jerusalem!" Our commander shouted, "But only after we burn this city to the ground! Not anything shall be alive in this city when we leave!"

"Charge," Someone shouted as we all went in, slaughtered women and children and we killed the livestock, burned buildings, the wall, everything. By the end of the day, it was destroyed.

"Now we attack Jerusalem!" Our commander shouted in the morning, as we all marched with him.

"Here we are!" He shouted. We saw a few hundred thousand men stationed in Jerusalem. It was so gigantic. I wonder how the Benjaminites feel about it. It's their possession, but we'll clear it out for them, or at least that's what our commander says.

"The Jebusites are coming!" Everyone was shouting as a wave of them attacked us, we easily sent a hailstorm of javelins on them and most of them were dead, while others were wounded. We quickly picked up our javelins and spears and we ran at the Jebusites. They didn't have any spears or javelins to launch at us, and no bows and arrows either, so we could easily launch spears and javelins at them, pick them up, and then throw that at another target.

"Breakthrough," Our commander shouted as we all went to the gate and destroyed their defences. There was nothing left to do, but the destroy the civilian's hope and crush them, if there was a rebellion, and then, just let the Benjaminites come in and take their city! Now, we are rid of Canaanites in our lands of Judah! Praise be to the Lord!

Judges 1

The Hammer and the Peg
Barak's View

"The Caananite King is coming!" Everybody was shouting. We knew that if we didn't respect him, our heads would be off. I saw that happen to somebody in the tribe of Dan, a few days ago.

We've had to work torturous hours for the Caananite King, Jabin. His ruthless commander, Sisera and he have oppressed us.

It all started when Israel started worshipping worthless idols, such as Baal and Asherah.

I've tried to talk my tribe out of it, but they don't believe me. One day, Deborah, the judge and prophetess that is teaching about the real God sent for me.

"Barak, the Lord has given me a vision." She said. I was confused.

"If the Lord gave you a vision, why would you send for me?" I asked.

"It is a vision concerning a battle with the Canaanites. The Lord wants you to be the leader of the Israelites in battle." She said.

"How many men should I take with me?" I asked. My head was swarming with questions to be asked.

"You shall take 10, 000 men of Israel with you, you will be victorious." She said.

"Where shall I meet the Caananite Army?" I asked.

"You shall meet them at the Kishon River." She replied.

"If you go, then I'll go." I told her, just to make sure that it wasn't some type of joke.

"Very well, but I must warn you that, even though you will succeed in battle, the credit for the victory will be given to a woman." She warned me. I was confused. The only woman going to battle was her.

"Barak, it's time to wake up!" My close friend said. He was also coming into battle with me. I had gained a recruit army pretty easily. Everybody wanted revenge on the Canaanites. Nobody likes them at all. I had to turn down about 1 thousand people, who came too late to join.

"Okay, I'll get up." I said, "Can you get the other men all to assemble in one big group, so I can bring them on to the Kishon River?

"Okay, got it." He hurried and left.

"Charge!" Sisera ordered as he and his numerous troops and chariots started coming. I shouted to defend.

"Ahh!" Sisera's troops shouted as suddenly, a storm raged and the side or the river that Sisera's troops were on flooded, killing more than half of them.

"Where is Sisera?" The rest of the Caananite Army was shouting, as they were getting cut down by our swords.

"Sisera fled on foot!" I shouted as we finished off the rest of the Caananite Army and we charged in pursuit. Soon, we split into groups. Then, I saw the tent of Heber, the Kenite. I wonder if Sisera's in there. I've heard that the Kenites were always allies of the Canaanites. Maybe they still are. Whatever happens, we have to find and kill Sisera. If we don't, we'll still be under Jabin's rule. Jabin is dependent on Sisera. Without Sisera, He would have no support for his army, and he would be conquered quickly.

"Hello, I am Barak." I introduced myself to a Kenite woman, and she didn't even introduce herself.

"Are you looking for Sisera?" She asked.

"Yes, as a matter of fact, I am." I said.

"Look inside." She said, pointing inside the tent. I looked, and it was a mess of blood and other things. It looked really nasty. At first, I couldn't tell who it was, and then, I saw the armour. It was Sisera. Heber the Kenite's wife had put a tent peg into Sisera's brain, while he was sleeping.

"We are free!" Everyone shouted. I learned that after the cruel Caananite King learned of Sisera's death, he and his head advisors fled back to their home land, only to find it destroyed and burned. Then, Deborah and I sang a song that praised the Lord, God of Israel for everything he did. All the Israelites repented, and we all had peace.

"Deborah?" I asked.

"Yes?" She replied.

"Do you think that Israel is going to be unfaithful to the Lord, after this?" I asked her.

"Perhaps." She replied.

Forty years have passed now and I was getting weaker. "My will is that my sons and daughters shall evenly split the share." I said, as I breathed one last time. Then, everything went blank and black. I was with the Lord now.

Judges 2-3

Aram Naharaim is Defeated
An Israelite's View

A few of us Israelites started to worship Baal and other Canaanite Gods. Therefore God, the one and only of the Israelites was angry at us. He sent many armies at us, and finally, the army of Aram Naharaim conquered us. We were all upset and our people were all scared, because Cushan-Rishathaim, King of Aram Naharaim was saying that if we didn't obey him, we would be his slaves forever. Nobody wanted to be a slave, because our ancestors were slaves in Egypt and I think that it must've felt more than just plain torturing, it must've felt like you were doing something for nothing.

"All you Israelites," Cushan-Rishathaim shouted at us, "If you don't let us listen to this! If you don't rebel against me and my fellow people from Aram Naharaim, then you will enjoy a life of comfort as subjects, but if you rebel, we've got no other way to do this, so we must put you into harsh treatment and harsh labour!"

"Yes, King Cushan-Rishathaim!" We all chorused, knowing those lines off heart from all the times we've said it. I wonder why we even say it. If we still worshipped our God, the one and only, we'd be out of Cushan-Rishathaim's hand. I tried to organize a group so that that the people would believe in him again, but I got little support. I had a few people like Othniel, brother of Caleb, the spy. But other than that, other people still believed in pagan idols like Baal, and Asherah.

Othniel is like a leader to the Israelites and if I could just get all the Israelites to turn back to God, the one and only God. I wonder why they don't do it earlier. I wish that I could make all the Israelites turn back. If they do, we won't have the yoke of Cushan-Rishathaim on our backs, telling us what to do.

"Othniel, will you help me?" I asked him as he looked at me and nodded. Then, he went to go have a speech to the Israelites about God. They looked astonished, as if they've never heard anything like it before. It looked like a few people didn't like the idea at all. They quickly picked their things and left to go live and bow to Baal and Asherah.

But others, who picked on pretty quickly, they went to go to Othniel to ask more questions. Finally, after that long day, we've been able to make almost all the Israelites revert to God, the one and only. I've breathed a huge sigh of relief since the Aramites have stopped most of their oppression on us.

Now, what we have to do is secretly raise an army and battle the Aramites for our rights and our God.

"Attack!" I heard Othniel shout. I tensed. Then, I just noticed it was only a drill. I'm so lucky that I was alert at that moment, because, suddenly, I heard a rumble. I knew it was the sound of chariots. I quickly told everyone, and they put away their weapons and then, we stood as if we were just looking around for something in the sand.

"We shall be going, the King expects us." The charioteers said as they went back to the Castle of Cushan-Rishathaim. They had helped us search for our lost golden bracelets.

We purposely hid the bracelets in the grounds, and so they found the bracelets, in a while. It was a pretty good scenario to play. If this ever happens again, we can just use this routine.

"Charge!" I heard at the tip of my ears. It was a riot between the Israelites. It took a few minutes to get sorted out. We had to finish off what they had started, by decreasing the likeliness of another riot.

"I think that the men are ready for a battle. We shall storm the chariots first, before they have any chance. We will destroy all their chances of winning. We will send decoy troops out, to get all the troops out of the City and we will destroy Cushan-Rishathaim's Empire in our rightful land." Othniel told me. I agreed with him, and so he made a speech and everyone was up to it.

"Charge!" Othniel shouted as he led a charge against the chariots. There were hardly any sentries, but we just killed them at first sight of us. We had been successful all the way. The whole entire battle was heated up. The archers from the palace started shooting at the decoy troops, but then, we stormed the palace. We snuck up on them and the battle was over. The Aramites fled from Israel. We were free!

"Thank the Lord!" Everyone was shouting down the streets of Israel. It was like a big celebration. We ended that day with a chorus of praises to the Lord the One God.

Judges 3: 9-11

Oxgoad to save Israel
An Israelite's View

"The Philistines are coming!" Everyone in town was shouting.

"You, Israelites shall be our slaves!" The Philistine generals were shouting as our army gave resistance, and was destroyed.

"You Israelites shall give us all your valuables and so on," The Philistines were saying as I ran for my life. I don't want to give my valuables. They're all on me, so I can just run out of this town, and hopefully find a safe place.

"Excuse me, what are you doing?" A Philistine soldier asked me as I ran out of the gateway. I didn't respond to them.

"Army, after that runaway!" They shouted as I ran for my life. Luckily, somebody running in armour isn't as fast as someone who has loose clothes.

"Phew, thank you, Lord, for letting me get away!" I praised the Lord, the one and only God. Ever since a little while back, a few tribes of Israel began worshipping foreign Gods, like Baal and Molech. My family and I, we decided to stay loyal to God, the one and only God, who is all powerful.

"Hello." I said to someone as I enter a walled town, called Hebron.

"Why have you come here today?" A few people asked as I entered hastily.

"The Philistines are coming." I said. They all panicked. Soon, a whole army of our soldiers came up on to the wall, with bows, ready to shoot the Philistines. But, the Philistines never came.

"What has happened to them?" Everybody was asking. They knew I wasn't lying about the Philistines. The Philistines have been raiding the Land of Judah for ages. Now, they want to take all of Judah.

"Let's go to see what happened." Everyone was shouting as I went out first to see what happened to the Philistines.

"Whoa, how come there are so many dead bodies?" Everyone was asking. There was a whole bunch of dead Philistines off to one side, and another pile on the other.

"How could somebody not suffer a casualty doing this?" Everyone was asking. I was confused.

"Run!" We heard. There was a few shouts and wails, then, we saw a few surviving Philistines running away.

"Is anyone here?" A few people were asking. All we saw was a simple farmer out in the place, he had an oxgoad in his hand. I was kind of made, because it looked like he was wasting a perfectly fine oxgoad for his oxen, which took a lot wood, which was scarce here.

"Why did you waste that perfectly fine oxgoad?" I questioned him.

"Did you want me to let Hebron be destroyed?" He asked. He had a very strong Caananite accent, but I knew that he had been part of Israel for a while.

"You're Shamgar, the Caananite aren't you?" Someone in the crowd asked.

"Yes, I'm Shamgar." He said. Looking at his clothes, he was probably really poor. He looked as if he had no food for a while, because he was thin.

"Do you know who killed all these Philistines?" An elder asked him.

"Yes, in fact, I do." He said. We all tensed as he opened his mouth to speak.

"It was I." He said. He picked up the oxgoad, and when I looked carefully, I saw the specks of blood. I knew that he had killed these Philistines with an oxgoad.

"You, with an oxgoad?" I said, "That's almost impossible."

"The Philistines will come again. If you don't repent to the Lord, then, you will be defeated." He said.

"What do you say?" I asked the rest of the people. I knew they really wanted the Philistines away, so they nodded.

"I will pray to the Lord." I said. I prayed to God, and asked for forgiveness. Then, I built an altar, and sacrificed a burnt offering.

"All you people, out there." I said, "You people have been saved by the Philistines by the one, the only God, for you have been given forgiveness, for all your wrongdoings in the past.

"The Philistines are coming!" A few people were shouting. I saw a few army men from Philistia coming over. I knew it was trouble. I immediately, went to Hebron, and there, I found Shamgar. He was more than willing to attack the Philistines. Instead of bringing a new sharp oxgoad, he brought the same one he used last time.

"Philistines, over here!" Shamgar shouted.

"Are you the person who killed my brother?" A Philistine asked. "I want revenge!"

"Charge!" A Philistine General shouted. They all charged on Shamgar. I was worried, but they circled Shamgar. Shamgar took his oxgoad, and spun in circles three times. He killed just about a whole section of them. Then, a few people dared to go 1 on 1 with him. Obviously, he crushed them, soon, after; the whole army of Philistines was lying in three piles.

"What happened here?" The Hebron people were saying as they came out of their gates, only to see about 10, 000 Philistines lying in piles.

"Shamgar killed them, once again, for God said he would." I said.

"Everyone, thank God, the One and Only!" I shouted and everyone was rejoicing and thanking God. Then, we rejoiced and we held a banquet. We knew that Shamgar was our new judge from God.

Now, it's been almost twenty years from the day we were liberated from the Philistines.

"What has happened?" I asked someone. I was looking around. I had to enter Hebron to sell crops. Everyone was sad. I knew something was wrong.

"Don't you know already?" They replied. I looked around. It sounded like a grave city. Nobody looked happy. Perhaps somebody died or something.

"No, I know nothing about what happens in this city." I said.

"Shamgar, the judge, is dead." They said, sorrowfully. Then, I felt a pang of sorrow in my heart. Shamgar had been one of my friends. Ever since the liberation, I was his friend. Now, he is dead.

"Bye, Shamgar!" We all shouted as he was put in his grave. There, we caught the last glimpse of him and knew that he was now with the Lord, living happily in heaven.

Judges 3: 30-31

The Israelites Call for Jepthah
Jephthah's View

"You, get out of our house! We don't want you here!" My half brothers shouted at me as I walked away.

They hated me because we had the same father yet not the same mother. I wish I wasn't their half brother. I was the son of a prostitute and their mother was a real person in society. They decided to kick me out of the house, once my father died. The elders told them that they could kick me out.

"Fine then." I said. I packed up my things and I headed to the land of Tob. First, I would have to pass the gate, with the elders there.

"I shall never have anything associated with you anymore." I told to the town elders. "You let my brothers kick me out."

They laughed. "It's like we'll ever need you." They taunted as they kicked me out of the gate and laughed as I stumbled down the road.

"God, please help me." I said, as I met people, who always stared at me.

"Yes, Jephthah, I'll always be with you." God whispered to me as I walked down the road.

"What are you doing?" A mob of men who were down the road were shouting.

"Just leave me in peace." I begged. Luckily, they followed my orders and did what I said.

"Jephthah, what are you doing?" A few of my father's friends were saying as they passed down the road. I ignored them and kept on walking, as if I were deaf to them.

"I'm finally here, Lord." I said as I dropped my things when I entered Tob. I found a nice little unsettled place, where I set up my house. I got some supplies and I started raising sheep. I can't wait until they're mature since they will provide food and perhaps clothing. That is, if I can find a seamstress in Tob.

"Why have you come here today?" I asked, as a few people, who looked like people from Gilead.

"We have come, to ask you to lead us into battle." They said. I was annoyed. I was as good as a soldier as I was before, but they didn't accept me before.

"Are you really going to accept me as your leader?" I asked. They nodded.

"Okay, then, if you say so." I said. I was still a little uneasy, but I don't really care.

"Jephthah! You are here!" The elders said as I walked in the front gate.

I looked at them.

"Why have you kicked me out before, and now ask me to help you in battle?" I asked.

"Well, that was history. Now, we want you as our commander." They said.

"Will I truly become your leader, even after this battle?" I asked.

"Yes, and we will promise by the hand of God." They promised. I was pretty ecstatic. If they promised that, it meant that I would be their leader into war and post-war.

"Okay. I will start right away." I said, I sent 2 messengers to the King of Ammon to ask why he was invading our border.

He already had the reasons written down on a piece of papyrus.

When Israel came out of Egypt,
They went on the east side of the Jordan,
From the Arnon to the Jabbok, used to be all of Ammon's Land.

All of us Israelites knew how big of a lie that was. Ammon was just trying to win land from us. From the Arnon to the Jabbok, to the Jordan, It was all King Sihon and King Og of the Amorites' lands. We successfully defeated both of them in battle, and so, we should have all the land.

"Messengers!" I shouted, "Go tell the Ammonite King, that we have done nothing of what he spoke of, and that we shall be ready for battle if he disagrees.

"Yes, Jephthah," They said as they hurried off into the desert sands.

"We are back!" The messengers reported as I looked at them.

"What news did the Ammonite King bring you?" I asked.

"He just made us go away, because he didn't want to listen.

"Okay, then, let him be that way!" I said. "Troops of Gilead, follow me!" I shouted. A whole mob of troops were there. I waited a while, then, I went, and I scouted and looked over the Ammonite camp once we reached near it. Then, as soon as I saw the defences were weak, I called my troops.

"God, if this attack is successful, then, the first thing that I meet once I get home, shall be yours, Lord.

I looked around. All the sentries were looking around. Since our men were hidden in bushes, the sentries couldn't see them .

"Charge!" I shouted. My troops were coming out of the bushes, firing arrows and slashing Ammonite sentries with swords.

"Surrender!" I shouted to the Ammonite King as he appeared in front of me.

"Yes, I surrender." He said. All of us Israelites partied. Then, I remembered my vow, I quickly went home. When I got there, I was met by my daughter and she was jumping around. Then, once again, I remembered my vow. I was filled with sorrow.

"My daughter, you will have to serve the Lord, the rest of your life, for I've made a vow to the Lord." I was full of grief.

"Father, it's okay. For if you've made a vow to the Lord, then, it shall be, but first, I have a request." She said.

"What?" I asked.

"That, my friends and I can go into the mountains to weep for 2 months, for I will never see them ever again." She said.

"Yes, you may go." I said. She immediately went to her friends' houses to go ask them to come. All of them went. I didn't see my daughter for another 2 months. Finally she came back.

"Father, now I shall go to serve God the rest of my life." She said, as she gave me a hug and headed down the road. I knew that she would live a life full of goodness and that she would please the Lord no matter the circumstances.

Judges 10-11

Jephthah and Ephraim
An Animal's View

I looked around. It was close to noon. Soon, I would eat my lunch. Suddenly, I found my way into a nice place, near a bridge to go find some grass to munch on. Suddenly, I saw a few hundred men that all looked the same; stand at the bridge. Then, they crossed the bridge. I was curious, so I went over.

I hid a bush to keep me under cover. If they saw me, they'd probably kill me for meat. My parents and brothers were killed for meat. I like to know things, but sometimes, I get in trouble for it. I saw my brother get fried and eaten. It was a horrible sight.

Anyways, back to the situation. The men crossed and looked as if they were trying to find somebody. I was scared. Maybe they were looking for me. Maybe they were hunting. That wouldn't be nice. Suddenly, I saw another bunch of men, who looked almost the same, but just a tad bit different, come over. I hope they're not coming together as a hunting party.

"Jephthah, why did you go to battle, and not call us?" A man asked. I sighed a sigh of relief. It wasn't a hunting party. It was merely just a plain old thing, where they were going to fight it out.

"I already asked you, before the battle even started. You didn't listen, so I went myself." The man named Jephthah said.

"No you didn't!" The first group shouted.

"Yes we did!" Jephthah's group shouted back. The First group raised their weapons but, Jephthah's army was too quick. They had it prepared. Their archers sent 5 volleys of arrows, and after that, almost all of the people who crossed the bridge were running.

Soon, I saw Jephthah, stationing people at the bridge.

For some weird reason, today, I was at the bridge, when I saw somebody trying to get past Jephthah's men.

"Are you from Ephraim?" They asked.

"No." The person said.

"Say 'Shibboleth," They said. I could see the person trying to cross was doing his hardest, but no matter what, he couldn't say it.

"Seize him!" They shouted. A few soldiers came out of nowhere and killed the person. I'm lucky I'm not that person. I would be running for my life by now. I'm lucky I've got long legs, to run fast. If I didn't, I probably would be meat by now.

"Jephthah, how many people have we killed so far?" Somebody asked the person named Jephthah.

"I think we've almost totalled one thousand." He said. *That's crazy!* I thought. I probably haven't even seen so many burrows in my life!

"How do you say Shibboleth?" Another one of Jephthah's guards was asking another unfortunate person.

"Sibboleth." The person said. He got a few people chasing after him, and then, I didn't want to look at the part, where he got a spear in his back. It was too bloody. It looked even bloodier than my mother's death. My mother got hit in the stomach, one time, by an arrow.

"Charge!" Somebody shouted. I knew it was an army that was crossing the bridge.

"Defend!" I heard Jephthah shout to his troops. His troops were ready, unlike the others. They shot arrows, and the army crossing ran away.

"That was easy." I heard Jephthah say, as he and his troops went back to his camp.

"Jephthah, how many prisoners have we seized now?" I heard a man say. I edged a little more curiously, to listen.

"We've seized about 5000 from the day we started, to now." Jephthah, answered as the people entered their camp.

"Jephthah!" One of his men shouted, as he came back from his guard patrol, on the bridge.

"Yes," He answered.

"We caught 20 people trying to raid over!" The man said, joyfully, as Jephthah looked pleased.

I looked around, for a nice place to lie down, when I saw a man on a horse racing by. I quickly got out of the way. One of my relatives was killed by horse.

He was just standing there, when a horse came by, and before he could react, the horse stomped on him. It was almost as bloody as the scene that I saw with the person with the spear in his back.

"What's this?" I heard someone from the Jephthah's army say. I knew something bad was coming. Then, I saw an army of those people, who I heard were Ephraimites, when I was listening to people in the camp.

Then, they ambushed the camp, but once again, Jephthah's archers proved effective and they destroyed a bunch of the men.

"What is the animal doing here?" An Ephraimite said, as he saw me. Before I knew it, he pulled his bow out, and loaded it with an arrow. I was so shocked, I didn't move until the last moment. I jumped just out of reach, of the arrow, and I got away.

"This filthy beast is harder to catch than I thought it would be!" The Ephraimite muttered as he started running away at the sight of Jephthah.

He called me a filthy beast! I thought, *I'm not a filthy beast, I'm a nice, kind animal I am definitely not filthy; I take a wash in the river every 2 days. I am not a beast either. Anyone could look at me, and think that I was the cuddliest animals on earth!* I didn't trouble myself with these thoughts when I heard more voices.

"Archers, shoot!" I saw Jephthah and his men advancing. It's almost been a month since the first fight. I need to rub myself against a nice bur bush to get rid of my long wool.

"Retreat!" I heard somebody from the Ephraimite side shout. The Ephraimites ran for their lives. Those who got away were fortunate. Only 100 of the original 500 got away.

"Jephthah, how many have we got now?"

"We've got about 42 thousand." Jephthah said confidently and proudly.

"Really?" His men seemed astonished. I heard myself jump. That was such a great accomplishment

It's been a long time since that day now, and today, all the people are mourning. Even I'm a little sad. Today is the day, that the great judge Jephthah died. I still remember a few years ago, defeating the Ephraimites. That was pretty amazing.

I also had the honour of having Jephthah buried in my own burrow. I don't care. I've already made another one. They're easy, and fun to make. Well, Jephthah is dead but we will always remember him to be a strong and mighty warrior in the name of God!

Judges 12

The Battle of Benjamin and Israel
A Little Child's View

"Father, what's going on around here? Everyone looks so worried and scared."

"Well, something bad has happened around here. There are very bad men in Benjamin. They killed someone's wife. Now, we are to muster an army and go attack the Benjaminites." Father told me

"But aren't they our friends and our relatives? " I asked.

"Well, kind of, but they aren't friendly with us anymore. They're hostile. They've sent messengers around, telling us that they are willing to declare war on us. They've already gotten ready 26,000 valiant swordsman and another 700 left-handed slingers that can hit just about any target that they choose." Father explained. I nodded.

"Are you going to fight?" My younger brother, Terah, asked my father.

"Yes, of course, it is a law that all men of Israel fight this battle against our relatives, the Benjaminites. It is a battle of justice, not a battle for land or anything, like livestock." Father said.

"Will Eliab go too?" I asked. I didn't want Eliab to go. He always stands up for me, and he's the only person who actually minds me in this village, other than Father, Mother and other family.

"No, he will not. They do not demand boys in the army. They do not want boys who are just going to kill themselves in battle." Father said.

"Are you saying that I will kill myself in battle?" Eliab challenged. We all laughed. Mother even laughed from, where she was.

My little sister, Tamar, has been sick for a long time, and she has been in bed for an even longer time. Now, Mother has to take all of her time and take care of her.

Now she has no time to do anything with me. She doesn't tell me one of those stories about the old ancestors. Tamar and I used to always just sit there on the sheepskin rug and listen to Mother as she told us stories about the battles of Israel and the Canaanites.

Mother has two things to worry about. Father, who's off to fight the Benjaminites, and little Tamar, who's so sick she can't get out of the bed she's lying in. I wonder how she can't. I thought. *I don't know anyone who can't freely get in and out of their bed. Maybe it's just that Tamar's disease is really rare. I wonder how she got it.*

"Is it really true that you are going to have to go away for a whole month?" I asked Father. He nodded.

"How much time do you have before you have to go?" Eliab asked.

"Tonight is the last night at home. Early tomorrow morning I will be gone." Father said, as tears streamed down our eyes and Father even started crying. We all wept and prayed to the Lord for guidance, and we all went to bed, for that night we all needed a good night's rest. It was almost midnight when we finally finished getting everything ready. After our talks, it was almost dawn.

"It's time to wake up!" Mother shouted. I noticed that we had slept until the afternoon, because the sun was heading to the west rapidly.

"Yes, Mother I'm coming!" I said as I quickly put my robes on and I ran towards the kitchen. It was filled of scents of oxen and cattle. I knew that Dad had slaughtered one today and now we were going to eat it. Then, I noticed that Father wasn't there, and I remembered he went to battle. Eliab must have killed the cattle then.

I wonder how Father is doing in battle the attack should have started. I've heard rumours that we have 400, 000 men while the Benjaminites only have 25, 700. I've also heard rumours that the people of Israel have the odds of 1 in 8 people killed.

"Rebekah!" I heard Mother shout. I noticed that my bread was leaving a lot of crumbs on the floor, while I daydreamed. Now, Mother makes me pick them up, and eat them, which is one of the most embarrassing tasks in the whole of our house. One time, she even made Father do it, which made him so embarrassed that he had to stop eating.

"Mother, can you tell me one of those old stories that I used to love?' I asked her. Usually she wasn't willing, but today, Tamar's been feeling unusually better and so, Mother's been going unusually nice today. She's been giving out treats to everyone.

Mother agreed and sat down next to Tamar and me and told a short story that even though we had heard it a million times, we loved hearing the story over and over again.

Knock knock! A messenger was at our door past the middle of the night. I quickly stumbled to Mother's room and I told her. She quickly scrambled to the door. It was someone from the army. They were dressed in full armour. The messenger looked sadly at Mother, and then started to speak in slow whispers. So soft that I couldn't hear him speak.

"What did he say?" I asked Mother. She looked at me with eyes filled up with sorrow.

"He told me that Father is dead. Or that they couldn't find him after the battle." Mother said, suddenly, tears streaming out of her eyes.

"Father is dead?" I asked.

"Maybe, he might be alive, but there is a slim chance." Mother told me. She quickly hurried me back to bed, and we waited for the next day to come. In the morning, Eliab and Tamar were asking what had happened, because they saw all the tears.

"Father might be dead!" I blurted out. They suddenly looked sad too. We all sat there, and cried, until we heard another knock on the door. This time, it was another messenger. The messenger once again whispered something quietly into Mother's ear.

"Your husband, has been found on the battlefield. He has sword wounds in his thigh, but that is all, he is to go back to your home, and recover there, until he is fit for battle." The whole family cheered as we read the news and later, as we were eating our lunch, Father came from a horse and knocked on our door. We ran excitedly. One, because of Father coming back, and the other because of the horse.

"Father, I'm so glad to see you!' I shouted as I leapt into his arms.

"Father, where did you get the horse?" Tamar asked, she, obviously was more interested in the horse.

"Well, everyone who was wounded draws a lot to see who gets a horse to ride. I just happened to win, and so here I brought it back. Father said as Eliab led it to the stable, and we all just went to the table and we ate.

"What happened the first day of battle Father?" I asked him.

"Well, there were 22, 500 soldiers of Israel killed yesterday." Father said.

"Wow, that's a lot." I said.

"Yes it was, but on the second day, only 18, 000 were killed." Father said.

"How did you know?" I asked him. He must've stayed in battle for a while.

"Well, while I was riding here and a messenger on a faster horse passed by. I asked how the battle went and he told me the details.

"Oh, okay." I said, as I headed to my bed, "I'm getting tired, I'm getting to bed."

"Yeah, so am I." Tamar said.

"Me too!" Eliab said as we all headed towards our bedroom, and we all slept.

It was morning and I woke to the sound of Father waking me up. "Time to wake up, guys!" Father shouted as we all kicked our blankets aside and we ran to go see everyone in the kitchen after we ate, and tended the horse and did all that we were supposed to. It was already evening when a messenger came and told us of the news of the battle. We had lost 30 men, and slain all but 600 men of the Benjaminites.

We all celebrated our victory, and we went to bed. I was so happy Father was home again.

Judges 20-21

Samuel

part four

Eli's Two Sons
A Priest's View

"Eli! Give your sons better punishment for the wicked things they do!" I heard Eli, our high priest talking with the Lord. Eli's two sons, Phinehas and Hophni, were the wickedest people I've ever seen.

They send servants from their rooms while people are sacrificing their animals, and it was a custom that the priests take a three pronged fork and take however much the fork had, but only after the fat was burned and sacrificed to the Lord.

But, Eli's sons sent servants before the fat was burned.

"No! You can't do it! The Lord will not reward you for all this!" I shouted at them, but they raised their forks at me, and they scared me, kind of.

"If you don't give it over, I will make you give it over to me." The servants said. It seems like they have practiced that line, over and over again, because they seem to scare me out of their wits. I quickly pray to God.

"Lord, please help me, for I am scared and I don't know what to do. I am only your mere servant!" I prayed silently.

"Just let them go, for I will give them proper punishment later, for they have disgraced my name in all Israel!" The Lord told me.

"Okay, I will let you, but you will pay the total price for it!" I shouted at the servants. They got the meat, and brought it to Phinehas and Hophni. I wonder what those 2 priests are turning these men into! I quickly did my work and when I had time, I went to check on the two priests.

"What do you suppose you are doing?" I asked Hophni, as he was in his bed trying to hide something, but I knew what he was doing. He was lying with one of the server women who were supposed to be virgins for their lives. When I tried to stop them, they ignored me and they threatened me with violence. I knew I should get out, so I did.

Then, I went to Phinehas' room. I wasn't surprised when I found that he was doing the same thing. I quickly reported to Eli, what they were doing and he went to go scold them. If they can withstand me, they can probably withstand their father. I wonder where they have learned such bad habits! Why would a priest of the Lord, defile the Lord's name so badly and also do things that people who aren't priests shouldn't do!

"You two, you shall listen to me! You are deceit and wicked in the eyes of the Lord. You have defiled the Lord far worse than any of the Lord's priests! For you have been wicked, and the Lord promises that he will destroy all the wicked in his sight," Eli shouted. I peered in the room. Phinehas and Hophni looked bored, like it was one of their father's normal speeches, like he says it every time they get together.

"We know, we know, but can't you let us live our own lives?" Hophni shot back at Eli, but Eli said nothing, but went out of the room and left those two in silence to talk among themselves.

I was eavesdropping by the door so I could listen to what they were talking about.

They were talking about how they did this, because somebody gave them money, and how they did that, because somebody gave them 50 oxen. They accepted many bribes and that was against the law in Israel. The Lord said that people who accept bribes will have to do two times the extra that they had to do, and they had to give back twice as much as they got from the bribe.

Then, the discussion changed. Then it talked about how one of them would be king and the other would be subject, and they kept on fighting. Finally, the situation got to a place where they both like it. It talked about what they ate. One talked about how the oxen fat meat was so good, while the other talked about how the lamb fat tasted better. I wonder how they could accept eating that. I think that eating fat is unacceptable. The only time I've had any fat was when there was a feast for us priests, and we had to slaughter our own animals, and have a feast. I had a bit of the fat.

It tasted gross. I wonder why it is considered the most luxurious part. It's so hard to chew and it makes you look plump. All priests aren't supposed to be plump. If you are plump, it probably means you've been stealing fat!

"The Philistines are coming!" A messenger shouted from the nearby land of Judah. The Israelites all prayed here and they went to go fight the Philistines. I went with the people to fight the Philistines. I was there to tell people and preach about God.

"Attack!" The Philistines shouted as they charged toward us. We sent a barrage, but most of those missed. I wonder how they missed, but then, the Philistines came at us and started inflicting heavy casualties on us. I ran away from the battle, because I was so scared. When I went to go count the dead, there was 4, 000 exactly. I wonder how many men will die tomorrow.

"Let's bring the Ark!" Everyone shouted. I went back to the gate of Shiloh and there, I saw Eli, dead. When I asked what happened, they said that while I was coming, the Israelites were defeated and that the Ark was captured and brought to Philistia! I almost fainted on that thought.

I thought the same about the ark as Eli did, but now, I think, it doesn't really matter, for the Lord is still in heaven, even if he isn't with us, here in the land of Israel. I'm sure that the Lord did this for a purpose and that purpose will show!

1 Samuel 1-4

The Ark Defeats the Philistines
A Bird's View

It all started when the Philistines decided to attack the Israelites. I knew it wouldn't turn out good for the Israelites, because I knew the Israelites were wicked and they defiled the Lord

"The Philistines are coming!" I heard the scared shouts of the Israelites, because they were scared of the Philistines, who had long knives, that they called swords and long sticks with points on top, that they called spears. I wonder who came up with such ironic names.

It's kind of weird, because one day, when I was flying over the island of Crete, I saw many people holding those, and setting places on fire. I wonder why they do it. I wonder why people kill. Why can't everyone live in peace?

Well, back to the topic. So that day, after the battle, the Israelites had been slaughtered. Four thousand men were killed n the fields, and nothing was gained. They were pushed back another few miles.

"Let us bring the Ark of the Covenant to defeat the Philistines!" I heard the Israelites shout as it was so loud that you could probably hear it all the way from Greece.

"The Ark is coming!" They shouted another few hours later. The Ark was brought. I quickly flew to Shiloh, where I saw Eli, the head priest sitting at the gate, because he was scared the Philistines were going to take it.

I quickly went back to my place on top of the battlefield, because it was the best view. I had to fight other birds to get such a view.

"What is happening?' the Philistines asked their leaders as the Battle lines were drawn. I laughed. I wonder how they didn't know about the ark of God, for it was the one and mighty ark that could destroy anything and it could glorify itself. The Philistine Leaders told them what it was,

So, the Philistines fought with all their might, and the Ark was captured. Now, the Ark, it first went to Ashdod, a City in Philistia. I fell asleep that night wondering what the Philistines were going to do with the Ark.

It's morning again! I'm going to go check on the ark. I wonder what's happened to it. I remember vaguely that the Philistines said they were going to put it in the Temple of Dagon. I'll go and check.

Alas! It is in there, and the funny thing is, Dagon, the Idol of Ashdod, is on the ground, and it looks like Dagon is bowing down to God! That's really funny.

"The priests are coming!" One of my fellow Birds shouted. I quickly scrambled out of the temple, and as I got out, I saw the priests of Dagon coming in. I stayed there in the window and I laughed as they looked so surprised.

Then, as people were coming in, they quickly put Dagon together and pretended nothing happened. By this time, I was chirping my head off.

I think the Philistines were annoyed of me so they sent two flaming arrows at me, but I dodged them easily.

"Come on!" The people shouted, as I fled through the sea. I landed on an island, which was deserted, well; at least it looked deserted to me. There was no one and nothing but a few trees in sight.

"Ah, a good place to rest." I said as I blanked out in my tiredness.

I woke myself up when I found the sun shedding its warmth on me. I fluttered my wings to go to see what happened in Philistia. I hope that the Philistines quickly give the ark back, because then, Israel would be back to normal.

I'm here, at the temple. I'm peering in the window. In it, I see something that is even funnier. This time, Dagon is on the ground, and his head is off, and so are his arms! Now I have a tale to tell. I can see that all the people are in severe pain right now. Apparently, a few other birds told me that they have tumours.

"Ahh!" I heard many people shout as they saw the sight of rats. Rats brought plague, disease, poison and fleas into cities. Rats were despised by almost every single person in the history of mankind. But to my friends, the ravens, they love rats because they could eat them all day, with having to be sick of them. I wonder how they would live on eating rats!

"Let's give the ark to our neighbours from Gath, for we don't want plague in our city, or we don't want anything disgracing our God, Dagon!" The People of Ashdod shouted as they moved the Ark to their neighbours, the people of Gath.

Now, while the Ark was at Gath, the Rats were drawn there, and also, the people there looked really painful. Everyone was holding on to their stomachs. It was really funny to watch them. Then, a plague of rats came. There were rats everywhere. The ravens didn't need to search for food. Their food was right there, in front of them. Then, the Philistines decided to move the ark to Ekron, but the people there blocked the gate, so they couldn't enter.

Well, so I went into Ekron and there, I saw the leaders of the Philistines having a meeting about where the ark should go next. Some people said for it to go back to Israel, while others say they should abandon it on a road.

The first one won, so they made 5 gold rats and also 5 tumours, for those were the things that were destroying the Philistines.

"We shall return the Ark to you!" The Philistines shouted, and the Israelites came to grab it, but just as that happened, the Israelites took their weapons and they attacked the Philistines, and the Philistines fled, for the Ark defeated the Philistines, once more time.

"Hurrah!" All the Israelites shouted as they praised the Lord for their victory over the Philistines!

God is all powerful! I know from that lesson. He doesn't need other people to clarify him. He can glorify himself.

1 Samuel 5

Ebenezer, the Rock
A Philistine Commander's View

"Ten thousand, twenty thousand, thirty thousand, forty thousand, fifty thousand, sixty thousand, seventy thousand, eighty thousand, ninety thousand! Wow, there are so many men! Have them in groups of hundreds of thousands." I said confidently.

My officers quickly got everyone in groups as I counted once more. "On hundred thousand, two hundred thousand, three hundred thousand, four hundred thousand – " I kept on counting until I reached a million men. One million men! That was the largest army I've ever commanded. I set my generals into order, got them ready, had my captains and army in order, issued weapons, and supplies, and then I went back to the base. The base was on top of a hill, so I could see what was happening in the battle.

I had my troops march into Israel and got into sight of the Israelite Army. We've conquered the Israelites a number of times, but we have always lost all our ground and driven back. I know one secret weapon they have; their God is all powerful, He destroyed us once, and he might again.

Now, we shall conquer them once and for all and destroy them, until they stop!

"The Philistines are attacking once again!" There were rumours starting, from the Israelites. I laughed as I commander my army at them in full force. We had many men, and they didn't look like an opposition.

"Charge!" I shouted to my troops. Our troops had a good order at first, but after that, there was a thundering boom. I could see why. In the background of the Israelites, there was a man, who was giving an offering on a altar, and he was praying. Probably their God again.

"Fall back!" I shouted. I don't think many people heard, because they just kept on fighting, but they were getting all slaughtered, one by one. I watched in a battlefield of blood. It was not a very pretty sight to see.

The few men who were still at camp I think are pretty lucky. I've sent a messenger to go and get them to fall back onto this hill. They'll be safe, because Gath is right behind us. We have many men ready in Gath.

"Fall back!" The message spread quickly. Half of my surviving men were into Gath by the time I got into there. The lightning in the sky was still very heavy, but, it only landed where we were, not where the Israelites where, so it was like, a barrage of arrows, so they can advance behind it!

"Defend!" I shouted. We out-numbered the Israelites, 7-1 in battle, so the odds were in our way, until a lightning strike hit our wall, the walls collapsed, and many died. I ran for my life.

Even when we reached Ekron, I kept on running. I knew I would be safe in Ashdod. That was the capital, and there was a big chance we would win.

"Phew." I sighed in relief as I got to Ashdod. I had a few dozen men with me. When the King of Philistia asked me what happened, I told him the unbelievable events that happened. I don't think he will fall into my true theory of what happened.

"You have not reached the rank of commander, now I can see, for you lack the wisdom and strength to even win a battle!" He said. "I will dismiss you now, before you have any more military engagement."

Just before he said that though, there was news that both Gath and Ekron had been taken back by the Israelites. Now there were only three districts. I laughed at the thought. I went by myself to a field that was allotted to me and I went there and started harvesting my crops. I had to do this by myself now, because I don't have the provided servants from the king. I went outside to harvest and that's when I saw a messenger with torn clothes. I asked him what happened and he said, Ashdod was raided and all were killed. I couldn't believe my ears! Even the King was murdered.

Now, I know the Lord's grace on me, for if I stayed there and was still a commander for the army, I would've been murdered too, and now, I shall go to Israel to repent to their God, and I shall settle there. I know now that he is strong and almighty. I have nothing to bring, so I won't bring anything.

I'm going to go to the person who was sacrificing to their God, and I will ask him what I can do to repent. Then, I will do my best in the new land of Israel. It is going to be so new to me, but I don't care if it's new or not. I just care if I can repent my sins and I can give my new life to their God.

Now, I'm old, and I've settled in, I feel like I've never been. Now I have my own herd of animals, instead of an army. I'm plentiful of crops. I have a wife. I have many children. Now I see how the Lord has blessed me so much!

1 Samuel 7

The Crowning of Saul
A Servant's View

"Where are the donkeys, Saul?" I heard Kish, my Master, ask his son.

"I don't know, I think they might've run off with the sight of green pastures over near Gibeah." Saul told his father.

"You shall go with the servant to go find them." Kish said as he filled up two bags with food, and he gave me a quarter of a shekel of silver to use if anything happened and we really needed the money.

"Okay! And now, we shall set off!" I said as we started walking towards the places the donkeys might've set off.

"It's been a full day and we still haven't found the donkeys!" Saul exclaimed. I was taken aback, because Saul never screams like that. I wonder how Saul did that, because he always seems to be under control.

"Well, our food sacks are still halfway through. We could search at least for another day." I told him brightly. He nodded as we got ready to sleep in a tent.

When it came to morning, Saul seemed tired. "Wow, its morning already!" I declared as we got up to search again. I wonder how we are going to find the donkeys, but when there is God, there is a way.

"Saul, our sacks are empty now." I told him as we finished lunch. I wonder how we are going to get back to Saul's house, because it took us one day and a half to get here, that means it'll be one day and a half to get back.

"Well, we'll see." Saul said as we went to pack up and get going.

"There's a city over there, where a prophet is, maybe he could tell you something." A person told us as we could go into the city.

"What shall we pay this prophet?" Saul asked, "For we have nothing, our food sacks are gone, and my father wants his donkeys."

"I've have the quarter of a shekel silver, that you could give him." I said as I handed the silver into Saul's Hands. He looked at it, and he nodded, as we continued.

Inside the gate Saul asked the first person he saw about the prophet.

"Do you know where the prophet in this town is?" Saul asked.

"Yes, I am who you are talking about." The prophet said. I noticed it wasn't just any person; it was Samuel, the famous prophet of the Lord, God almighty!

"I'm here to ask you about where our donkeys have gone." Saul said. He gave Samuel the quarter shekel of silver, but Samuel refused to take it.

"I am a prophet, not a fortune-teller." Samuel said. I looked him in the eye, and he looked like something forbidding was going to happen.

"You and your servant there shall dine with me, and we shall further discuss." Samuel said as he went and prepared a meal, and then he said I could sit on the table with them.

It was the first time sitting at a table eating. At first I couldn't believe it. At home, usually I would have to sit on the floor and eat scraps of food. Now, I get whatever I want! It was luxurious!

"I have come here to tell you two things. One is that your donkeys are safe, and the other is that God has selected you to become the new King of all Israel." Samuel told me.

"What? How can that be? For my tribe, Benjamin is the smallest and my clan is the weakest, and my family is worthless in the clan." Saul muttered. I never knew that, for I thought Benjamin was a great tribe, for it always looked really large to me.

"What the Lord says goes, for he is the almighty, the strength of Israel, and he can make anything happen." Samuel said, as Saul kind of looked kind of confused. I wasn't confused at all.

"There are the donkeys, go bring them to your father, and in a few days, come to Gilgal and meet me there, for there I will crown you as King there.

"Yes sir, if the Lord says so, I will do as he wishes." Saul said as he got anointed by Samuel there, on the spot and then he and I went with the donkeys back home and then, he got ready to go to Gilgal. After that, we all crowded him, and I became a chief steward for him and everything seemed just right!

Praise the Lord for all he has done, for now, I am old, and my death is drawing near. I have seen what has been happening throughout the years, and now I am ready to go and have peace with God!

1 Samuel 9

Nabal, Abigail and David
A Messenger of David's View

"We have come to the pastures of Nabal, a flock-keeper!" David shouted, "We shall not touch or steal anything, and now that it is sheep shearing time, we will circle around all the sheep, so they may be protected and they may not escape!"

That is a pretty hard job, and it takes us hours just to get into order and to do David's orders.

"How are you doing?" I asked a buddy, who was right beside me.

"I'm not doing that well. Our food supply is going down, so I get less food, because I am a soldier, and messengers get more food." He told me.

I didn't tell him that he was just making too big of a fuss about it. It was true. We messenger have to be able to run fast, and if we don't, it doesn't work at all. A lot of people wanted to be messengers, but now, they know it is hard work, and that the only reason we have to eat a lot is because our hard work.

"Hello, I hear your name is David, thank you for setting up your men in a circle so our sheep can't get out, you should tell the master, Nabal, all that you have done, because you have been gracious." A shepherd told David. When he said that, I couldn't believe what he said.

"Okay, I will send ten messengers, who volunteers?" David asked. I shot my hand up quickly. I was the only one who raised me hand.

"Okay, You, and I will pick nine others, but because you volunteered, I will give you a special gift when you come back." David said.

He chose another 9 men and we headed off to greet Nabal, and tell him what we had done, and to kindly ask him for some supplies, because we were running really low on supplies. Now, our ration was one loaf of hard bread per meal and a bit of lamb meat and cheese to eat.

We've finally reached their house, I knock on the door, and Nabal comes out.

"What do you want?" He says in a gruff voice. One of the people draws a sword, but quickly sheaths it again.

"We are here to talk the word from David, son of Jesse, in the tribe of Judah, 'When your shepherds were with us, we did not hurt them, and at the time we were with the flock, nothing of the shepherds' was missing. Ask your own shepherds and they will tell you what we just told you. So may you please be favourable toward my messengers, for we can't spare one man. Please give your men and your servant David what food you have left over.'" I said. Nabal just laughed at my remark and he didn't even bother to go and grab anything.

"Here's what I want you to tell this David, son of Jesse, 'Who are you, and why should I give meat that was slaughtered for my servants to you, for I do not even know who you are!'" He insulted David in front of us. We quickly scurried back to our camp and told David what Nabal had said. When David heard what he said, he went in front of the camp, and raised his sword.

"Unsheathe your swords!" He shouted. We all did. Then, suddenly, out of nowhere, Abigail, the wife of Nabal came out riding with donkeys. They had them full of supplies. It was so full that I couldn't believe my eyes. It looked like David was staring affectionately at Abigail.

"We shall feast tonight!" David declared and we all sat down on the cool green pasture and waited for our turn to get the platter to eat. It was a unfair but fast way to eat, because we can't waste time around here. We have to sleep early, so we're alert in the morning. Being alert is mostly all that matters.

"Now we shall have a good night's sleep." David said. We kept on having feasts and having early sleeps for the next week, or as it was scheduled we would.

It's already been a week since Abigail came. Now our supply is still streaming and high. Suddenly, a servant started riding towards us with news. I was scared for a moment because I was afraid that something bad was happening, but we just had to wait and have high anticipation for what happens.

"Nabal, the owner of this property has died from the hand of God. His sheep will go to his chief steward. Is there anything that you would like to report?" The servant said.

I thought and thought of what David might say, and what he said didn't surprise me.

"Will you go ask my faithful servant Abigail if she may be mine?" David asked and the servant nodded.

Abigail came riding, minutes later, and she said yes. Now, I know how strong the power of God is. Because Nabal was so wicked, God made sure that he would die!

1 Samuel 25

The Gibeonites Avenged
An Old Tree's view

"Where has the king gone?" I heard one of the Gibeonites shout at a guard. The Gibeonites, I still remember from the time of Joshua, the Gibeonites deceived him and the Israelites into letting them not kill them. Now, a few years ago, before King David was crowned King, evil King Saul decided that only Israelites could live in Israel, so he decided to murder all the Gibeonites. He didn't get the last few and now, the Gibeonites are once again plentiful. Now, the Gibeonites are looking for revenge. I wonder what they are asking for. I hope it's nothing to do with death.

"What are you doing?" I heard a guard from King David's Royal Guard coming over.

"We want revenge on the family of Saul, for he murdered our fathers, mothers, brothers, sisters, and so on." They said.

"For that reason, I will bring you in." He said. Now, that I'm almost 1 thousand years old, I am growing rapidly, and I can see into the Throne room with my height. I can hear almost anything, from about 100 metres away, so I can probably hear what they are saying in there.

"Hello, and what would you like?" King David asked them. I'm sure I can hear now.

"We would like revenge, for our parents, grandparents, brothers, sisters, aunts, uncles, and so on that have been killed. We want permission so we can kill one member of Saul's Family, per each thousand of us killed before." They said. I was petrified. It was something about killing.

"I remember," King David said. He was staring up into the sky.

"Will you help our cause?" They asked.

"Yes, as a matter of fact I will," King David said. I was horrified. I never knew that King David would do such a thing. But, also, if he didn't do it, he would be called an unjust ruler, and the Gibeonites, would probably rise against him and his family.

"How will you count the revenge, do you want one for one, or two for one?" King David asked. I was shocked. I was so shocked, I didn't move my branches, even when the warm wind passed and fell on my back.

"We don't want much," They said, "We want one per one thousand."

"Okay, then, how many Gibeonites were killed?" King David asked. I've recovered now. My branches are shaking and I'm shivering from the cold wind. My branches feel as if they're about to fall off.

"There were roughly about seven thousand Gibeonites killed." They answered.

"Well, then, seven people from Saul's Family shall be executed." King David said. Immediately, a few of his scouts came out of the stables, with horses and went out to seek Saul's Family. In no time, Saul's family was found, and 7 members were brought there. I recognized their faces immediately. They were; the two sons of Rizpah, who married Saul and the five sons of Michal, the daughter of Saul. I didn't want to look at the killing of them, but when you're so tall, and when you're standing still, it's hard not to see it. I saw what happened. A few Gibeonites took ropes, tied them up and took swords, and charged. None escaped. It was really bloody.

When I looked at the aftermath, all of Saul's descendants had blood and guts pouring out of their bodies.

There is a large hole in every single one of their stomachs and all of them have bits of blood and guts flowing out every once in a while. It was so painful watching them that I didn't want to see them anymore.

I wish that I'll never witness anything like this again. It is just too much for something like me to see. I wish that I could fall down and save those people. Seeing people die is one of the worst things I've ever seen.

If I ever had one wish, it would to see no more people die. Some people, after they killed a person, they lay the person right at my trunk, to rot. It is gross. Every single day, a new wave of bugs would crawl on him every single night.

I don't know why King David chose this site to kill the people. I wish he chose another site, so I wouldn't have to see all of this. If I didn't see any of this, then I would've had a peaceful day, eating the warm sunlight and drinking the cool warm water, and turning my leaves green. I wish I had my leaves every single day of the year, for then I would remain looking good, even in the winter.

Anyways, the people who were killed by the Gibeonites, were taken, (to my advantage) and dug a hole and threw them into a pit. The blood was still there from the place where they were killed. Then, I heard the group of Gibeonites cheering, shouting, "THE GIBEONITES HAVE BEEN AVENGED!" They shouted. I knew that they had, for 7 of King Saul's descendants had been killed for the 7000 that King Saul had killed before.

2 Samuel 21: 1-14

Kings

part five

The Ravens Bring Food
Elijah's View

"The Lord declares that there will be drought and famine in this land of Israel!" I said fearlessly in front of King Ahab, the King of Israel.

"Enough!" King Ahab was furious. "Guards, seize him!"

God had told me to run to a place called the Brook of Kerith, that was across the Jordan River and that I should live there in secret for the rest of the famine. The guards, who obviously were going slower with their armour and soon, they disappeared out of sight.

"God, thank you!" I thanked God, as I saw that the guards were nowhere in sight. I usually have really close calls, but I've never been caught. A few of my fellow prophets, though, weren't so lucky. They either got their heads cut off, or other cruel happenings.

"Is this the place?" I asked God. I know it must be somewhere close. I've already crossed the Jordan, but I'm not sure that I've got the brook. I might have a fresh supply of water, but where am I going to get my food? Maybe this drought wasn't such a good idea after all.

"Yes it is here." I heard God whisper into my ear. I settled down. I saw the brook it looked cool and refreshing after such a long travel.

"Lord, thank you for the water, and the brook and protecting me, but where will I get my food?" I prayed.

"It shall be provided." A faint whisper in my ear was there.

I looked around, it was almost night time. I quickly had a drink and then I lay down in the sand and began to sleep.

That morning, I was amazed. I thanked as I saw that ravens were coming over my way. They had bread and meat in their beaks. They gave all of it to me.

"I told you I would provide, Elijah." God answered.

Soon enough, the drought had dried the brook up.

"Lord, the water in the brook is empty, for the drought has brought no water and it dried up." I complained. It's been about a year or so since the drought started, but now, all the water is gone.

"Elijah, go to the town of Zarephath near Sidon, where a widow will feed you." God said.

"As I approached the town gate, a woman was gathering firewood.

"Can you spare a drink of water for me?" I asked the woman. As she was going to get it, I asked her to bring me some bread too.

"All I have is a cupful of flour and a few drops of olive oil in a stone jar. I came here to find what little wood I could, to bake one last meal for my son and me. After that we will starve to death." She said.

"Do not worry." I said. "Go ahead and prepare a meal for yourselves. But before you do, bake a small loaf of bread and bring it to me. Then use the rest of the flour and oil to feed yourself and your son. Trust me, for the Lord, the God of Israel says, 'The cup will not run out of flour and the jar will not run out of oil until the day on which I, the Lord, send rain from the sky.'"

The widow followed my instructions, and all three of us had enough food for days. Just as the Lord had told me, there was always just enough oil to feed is all.

"Thank you Lord, for this day, thank you for giving me strength, thank you for protecting us. Please give me wisdom. Thank you for letting the oil and the flour never run out. Please help these people of Israel and please forgive me for my wrongdoings. Amen." I prayed.

Suddenly, one day, she came up to me in fury. "Man of God, why did you do this to me? Did you come here to remind me of my sins and so bring about my son's death?" She asked. Then, I saw it, her son was lying limp on the floor.

For once, I was speechless. The widow stared at me accusingly until finally, I said, "Give the boy to me."

I carried the boy upstairs, to the room I was staying in, and I prayed to the Lord.

"O Lord, my God." I prayed, "Why have you done such a terrible thing to this woman? She has been so kind to me, and now you have rewarded her by killing her son."

I prayed like that for three times. Suddenly, there was stillness. Then, I heard something. It was the child's breathing.

The child sneezed 7 times, and then got up. He walked right to his mom, and hugged her.

Tears filled her eyes and she said to me,

"No I know for sure that you are a man of God and that you speak the truth." Then, as the Lord had commanded me, I said farewell and I left them.

1 Kings 17

Ahaziah's Sickness
Elijah's View

One day, while I was working on telling the Israelites about the one and only God, the Lord told me to go up to a road that was from Samaria to Ekron.

He told me to go and say to the group of messengers sent by the King of Israel to say to their King, "Is it because there isn't any God in Israel that you sent messengers to go ask the God of Ekron for help?" When the people came, I sent them right off back. I don't know what happened, but I'm pretty sure that the King knew that it was me who told the messengers that. I think that he's going to send something to get me down to him.

It's another fresh day today. I was praying to the Lord last night, and he told me that there were going to be captains sent by the King. All I have to say is, if I am a man of God, then, let fire come down from heaven and consume you!

I've been waiting for so long now. Finally someone has come! It's an army captain. He has with him, 50 men.

"Why have you come here today?" I asked the captain.

"I have come to speak the words for the King! He says for you to come down immediately!" The man shouted.

"If I am a man of God, then, let fire come down from heaven and consume you!" I told the captain. Suddenly, a blaze came from heaven and burned them to crisp. When the fire finally was smothered, the remains of the men were nothing but a few bones and blood on the ground. There wasn't one survivor. Now, a second captain came with his fifty men a few minutes later. I knew what the Lord had said I should do. This time, the captain looked tougher than the last one. He looked like he wanted to hurt me and turn me into fried meat or something.

"Man of God! If you have true powers, than come down here!" The captain shouted. The Lord didn't tell me anything, so I guess I will do what I did to the first captain to this captain.

"Well, if I am a man of God, then, let fire come down from the skies and burn you!" I shouted. The fire didn't come as soon as I thought it would. The fire didn't come down until a little later. In that short while, the men started laughing and their captain started so chuckle. A few men even tried to attempt to climb the mountain. Suddenly, all was silent. Fire came down from the skies. The whole entire ground turned on fire. I was almost caught in the unbearable hot flames. I quickly got back into one of the caves and I started praying to the Lord. Before I could say anything, the Lord gave me instructions on what I should do when the third captain came to get me.

"Elijah, this time a third captain will come. He is not harmful to you. Go with him to the King's Palace. There, you will tell the King that he will not recover because he went to go consult Baal-Zebub, the God of Ekron." The Lord told me as I prayed.

"Yes, Lord. I will do that, for I am your servant and I will follow you all of my days, until you take me up to heaven." I said to the Lord. Then, I waited outside for the third captain to come. While I was waiting, I saw all the bones of the 102 men littered and there was some blood in spots. It was not a very pretty sight. I wish I couldn't see it, but I had no choice but to stay there and look at the bodies.

This time, the captain was a tall, slender man. His face looked scared. I stood on the mountain. I couldn't think of anything to say, but, he said something.

"Man of God! Please will you have respect on the lives of me and the fifty men with me. The two captains before went up before you and they were all burnt by the fire. Please will you just spare us, and come with us to the palace!" The Captain begged on his knees. I was just about to say what I said to the other captains, but then, I remembered what God said and I went with him and his men and we started walking to the palace.

Well, so we were walking to the palace when there was a dead bird on the ground. It grossed out half of the men. I just walked around it. A few men begged me to heal it, so I prayed to the Lord to heal it, and the Lord did heal it. The bird suddenly started to flap its wings, although it couldn't fly. The bird was just a little bird. One of the men decided to keep it as a pet.

"We have reached the palace! It's about time. It's been about an hour and an half or so. I've been scared that the King would have my head off if I told him the bad news.

"Hello, Elijah. What is the news from your God?" The King asked me weakly. He was still in his bed, lying there, and he was almost sounding like he would die soon.

"There is bad news, from the Lord, the almighty. He says that you will not recover because you have consulted Baal-Zebub, the God of Ekron instead of him, for he is Almighty and he is the only God of Israel. It is certain that you will die!" I shouted. The whole entire place turned gloomy after that.

Everyone was preparing for the King's burial. The third captain went all teary-eyed.

"The King has died!" The messengers were reporting. He had died in his sleep, during the night. The Lord's prophecy to me about Ahaziah was true and Ahaziah was never cured of his sickness.

2 Kings 1: 1-18

Ahab's Family Finished
Jehu's View

"The Lord says 'You have to finish off the family of Ahab." The Prophet said as he anointed me as King. It's really crazy. Me, as a King? I can't imagine it.

"Who wants to put Ahab's family's reign to an end?" I asked a few of my fellow friends. All of them raised their hands.

"We shall go!" I said. I summoned a messenger, to tell King Joram, Ahab's son, to meet me by Naboth's Vineyard.

"When the messenger came back, he also said that Ahaziah, the King of Judah was also there. What a surprise. Now I can kill all three remaining members of Ahab's family, without having to cause an uprising in Judah.

I drove my chariot to the vineyard gate, and there I saw the two Kings. I had my bow and arrows hidden. I also had a sword, just in case I needed hand in hand fighting. My small group of friends were behind me and they were the ones who were going to attack, if I died.

"Do you come in peace?" Joram asked. He looked kind of scared. I'm sure I'm not going to need my sword. He doesn't have any armour on. This might be an easier fight than I thought it would be.

"How can I come in peace, when Israel is full of witchcraft and Idol worship, all thanks to your evil mother Jezebel!" I shouted as I drew my bow and arrows.

"Treason!" Joram shouted. He drew his chariot, but I fired a quick arrow. He went limp in less than a moment. The arrow must've pierced his heart, because he looked like he had had pain in the heart suddenly. He clutched his heart. I hope Ahaziah doesn't have any armour either.

"Chase him!" I pointed to Ahaziah and shouted to my friends, who looked like soldiers in their armour and their swords. He was going full speed, but, I know that if I keep a consistent pace, I'll catch up to him soon.

"I'm going to shoot you!" I shouted as I shot an arrow that hit his chariot. Suddenly, his horse stopped. My men and I took the opportunity and we went full speed, caught up, and we killed him with swords.

"We shall ride to Jezreel next, and we shall kill the wicked Jezebel for she was the one who brought idolatry and witchcraft to Israel." I shouted to my men. We rode there in a few hours, and when we got there, I saw a woman, who had overly put cosmetics on. I knew it was Jezebel.

"Have you come in peace, you murderer?" She asked from the window. I looked inside. There were two or three eunuchs inside.

"Throw her out the window, or I'll have your heads!" I threatened.

They threw her out the window, and her blood splattered everywhere.

I rode over her with my chariot. Her body didn't look so pleasant when I rode over her.

"I'm going inside the palace to eat." I said to my friends as they happily went in with me.

"What happened to Jezebel's body?" One of my friends said, as all we could see was bones scattered, not even a single drop of blood.

"It was to fulfill the Lord's prophecy. That Ahab's family would be all killed, and their blood would be licked up by dogs, and their bones would be scattered so nobody could put them together." I said.

"Is there any more people we need to kill?" One of my friends asked.

"Yes," I said, "There are seventy more people in the house of Ahab that are in Samaria. I will send a message to the elders. If they will not kill the seventy, then, we will kill the seventy and them.

"Look, over there!" Someone shouted as we saw a group of 42 people arriving from the south.

"What are you doing?" I asked them.

"We are visiting Ahaziah, and his family." They said.

"Men, kill them!" I shouted. My men sprang into immediate action. They killed all 42. There were no survivors.

"Messengers have come!" I shouted as I saw the messengers. They were carrying a few baskets each, each with a head in the,

"The Elders have killed the 40 sons, and here is proof." The messengers said, as they put the baskets down. I counted. Exactly 70.

"I shall storm Samaria and I shall kill all Ahab's close friends!" I shouted as we drove to Samaria and I killed every single one of Ahab's friends.

Then, I got a lot more supporters, and I also asked all the people of Israel to come, as I said I was going to make a big sacrifice to Baal. I really wasn't going to. I just wanted it to be a way, to gather all the prophets of Baal, so I could kill them.

"I shall make a burnt offering." I said, as I pulled out 2 bulls and sacrificed them. Then, I gave the signal for my men to attack.

"Kill all of them!" I shouted. "Don't spare even one!"

Obviously, the people of Israel had no idea what I was saying, because I said I was going to make a sacrifice, but I ended up killing the prophets of Baal.

"Why did you kill them?" A few asked, "They were talking the truth." I ordered my men to kill those people. They were still loyal to Baal, a fake iron God, not the true God, a strong and powerful God, who reigns over everything.

"Do you see what happens when you defy the name of the Lord?" I asked. "I, am a supporter of the sole, living God, and if there is a person in the crowd that isn't, you will surely die by the sword of my men." I said. I made my people go to their homes and pray for their wrongdoings. Then, they would have to report back to me. If they didn't, they would die by the sword. After that day, I established my reign over Israel, and Ahab's family, along with the priests of Baal, were all massacred.

2 Kings 9: 13-37

Prophets

part six

Isaiah the Prophet
Interview

Isaiah the prophet prophesied against Israel and Judah for their wickedness. He often related the Lord to an eagle, taking us under the eagle's wing for protection.

Q: Hello, Isaiah, my name is Jasper, may I come in to interview you?

A: Sure, it would be a pleasure to tell you what I have learned.

Q: So, I would like to ask you why you even started becoming a prophet.

A: Well, it started first of all, when I was called by the Lord to prophesy for him.

Q: So, I'm guessing that you did, follow what the Lord told you to, or else, I'm guessing that you wouldn't have been a prophet?

A: Well, yes of course.

Q: While you were called by the Lord, did you hear his voice? Was it loud or was it a soft whisper?

A: Well, it was loud and it hurt my ears. I didn't dare cover my ears while he was speaking, so I just kept quiet.

Q: Did you see anything unusual when you were called?

A: Well, not really.

Q: I understand that the prophecy of the eagles is one of your most important prophecies.

A: Yes is it.

Q: Can you tell me a bit about it then?

A: Sure. So, first of all, it says how the people of Judah were being wicked in the eyes of the Lord.

Q: Yes, and then what happens?

A: Well, so then, it adds that only the Lord is all powerful and almighty. He will never be tired. He will never fall as he's walking.

Q: After that?

A: Well, so then the Lord mentions me to tell the people of Judah that even the strong and mighty can't even withstand long walks, and the young can't either. They will always grow weary while they walk. They will always grow tired and be forced to stop.

Q: What does the Lord tell you then?

A: Well, he tells me to tell the people of Judah that only the Lord will never grow weary and that they should repent.

Q: Was there any benefit? If there wasn't, I'd doubt anyone would want to repent.
A: Well, the Lord told me to tell them that the benefit was that they would have renewed strength.

Q: Yes anything else?

A: They would also soar like eagles in the air, because eagles never grow weary, however many miles they travel.

Q: Was there anything else?

A: They were that you could walk and never be tired, and run and never faint.

Q: But isn't there a limit to physical strength?

A: Well, it didn't really mean that in physical way. It meant that in a spiritual way.

Q: What do you mean by that?

A: I mean that people during their spiritual life, it is like some people grow weary and they don't want it anymore.

Q: Oh, I see. What about the renewed strength part?

A: Well, it's kind of hard. You will have new strength in your spirit and you won't grow weary of your spirit.

Q: Okay, I can see now.

A: Is there any other things you would like to ask about me before it's too late?

Q: Well, are there any other prophecies that you prophesied about?

A: Well, there are ones that I prophesied against other nations like Ammon, Edom, Moab, Tyre, Lebanon, Aram, Philistia.

Q: What were they even about?

A: Well, a few of them were how they were going to be punished for all their wickedness and a few others were about how they were going to be lamented by other nations.

Q: Is there anything else you can tell me?

A: Well, there was a few prophesies telling about how Judah and Israel would be punished and destroyed because of their horrible acts.

Q: What were their horrible acts?

A: Well, there was adultery, murder, stealing, lying and other things forbidden.

Q: Thank you for your time, Isaiah.

A: You are very welcome. It was my pleasure to answer your doubts and questions. Blessed be the Lord who warned me about these people.

Isaiah 1-66

The Bones of the Valley
Interview

Ezekiel was a prophet in exile, who dreamt of the dry bones becoming flesh.

Q: I understand that the Valley of Bones was one of your most important prophecies, isn't it?

A: Yes, it was, as a matter of fact. Do you want me to tell you a little bit about it?

Q: Yes, of course.

A: Okay, so first of all, the Lord, the God, one and only told me to be a prophet in his name.

Q: Well, I'm guessing you did become one, right?

A: Yes, I did.

Q: So, then what happened after that?

A: God sent me a vision.

Q: What was the vision?

A: It was that I was standing on a hillside, and down under where I was standing was a whole valley of thousands of skeletons.

Q: What happened after you saw all those skeletons?

A: Well, first of all, what happened was God's voice appeared again.

Q: What did he say?

A: He told me to preach to the bones.

Q: I don't exactly get how you can preach to dead bones.

A: I know. I didn't get it either. Then, God said that the people of Judah and Israel were the thousands of bones.

Q: Ah, now I see. Okay, so did you preach to them?

A: Yes I did, but I didn't exactly preach. I'm a prophet so I give prophecies.

A: Okay. Another of my questions is that were you scared when the Lord talked?

Q: Yes, of course.

A: What did the voice sound like?

Q: It was like thunder, booming into your ears. It hurt my ears really badly.

A: Okay, and did you see anything amazing in the vision that you got from God?

Q: Well, after the Lord told me to preach to the Israelites, the skeletons suddenly started forming into bodies. There was skin and blood in the people. There was also a loud rattling noise.

A: Did the sound kind of sound like a rattlesnake's rattle?

Q: Well, yes, of course, don't all rattles sound like a rattlesnake?

A: Well, yes. Okay, back on topic. I've got another question.

Q: What is it?

A: Well, my question is that if you had any other visions and prophecies.

Q: Well, of course yes. What do you think?

A: Okay, can you tell me a few.

Q: Okay, well. A few of them were all the same basis. They all talked about hostile nations of Israel and how their downfall would be, and why they were so arrogant and things like that.

A: Okay, any others?

Q: Well, there were a few about why Israel went to Israel and that they would soon return to their homes because the Lord was gracious with them.

A: Well, I'm guessing there are more prophecies that you've prophesied, aren't there?

Q: Well, there's the one about false prophets.

A: Well, what is it about?

Q: Well, it's talking about how they falsely tried to imitate the prophets of the Lord, and how they would be punished.

A: I think I've heard something about false prophets before.

Q: Well, my good old friend, Jeremiah, also talked about false prophets and how they would make you weak in the gospel and how they tried to lure you into evil things.

A: Okay, is there anything else you'd like to tell me about?

Q: Well, there was another prophecy; it was about Gog and Magog.

A: Who or what are they?

Q: They're supposed to be princes.

A: What does that have to do with anything?

Q: Well, the Lord told me to tell the Israelites that Gog and Magog would gather up men from all the far corners of the earth.

A: Wait a second, but the earth is not square!

Q: Well, you can't blame the biblical people, they were ancient. They probably didn't even know a thing about how a telescope works.

A: I see…

Q: So, then, they would fight against the Lord and after that, the Lord will have victory, but all the people died and he also said to me that after that battle, the Lord would unleash several events that harmed the world really badly, and that would be known as the end of the world.

A: Really? So the book of Revelation should say the same thing, right?

Q: Well, Revelation is way more detailed than what the Lord told me.

A: Okay I see. Is there any other prophecies?

Q: Well, there's one about how I was going to be a watchman.

A: I don't get why you would be a watchman.

Q: Well, it's because I had the job of warning Israel and Judah about their captivities.

A: So, I'm guessing that you got that before captivity.

Q: No, I didn't, it was about warning them when they came back. I was to be their watchman and warn them about the hardships.

A: Okay, I see, and did you have any specific pressure?

Q: Well, yes, because before that, the voice of God came to me and told me that it's just like if there was a war. If the watchman sees the enemy coming and blows the trumpet, and the people hear it and don't react, it's the own fault of the people. But, if the watchman sees the enemy coming and does not blow the trumpet, rather just run away, all the deaths will be the watchman's fault.

A: Okay, I get it; I can see all the pressure loaded up on you.

Q: Yes, but, I kept on pushing and the Lord helped me through.

A: I can see that. The Lord must have encouraged you so much during your hardships. Did you ever doubt the Lord when you were going through these times?

Q: Sometimes, I would have the slightest feeling that God didn't know what he was doing. But in the end, I knew God was almighty and faithful to every one of his believers just like he was with me.

Ezekiel 37: 1-14

The Writing on the Wall
A Babylonian Official

As an official to King Nebuchadnezzar, I enjoyed the privileges of a comfortable living in the Castle.

However, to my chagrin, he was killed and his son, Belshazzar became the King of Babylonia and its provinces. However, instead of being put to jail and executed like many other of my old master's officials, I had the privilege of being placed as the chief advisor to the King.

Soon after, Belshazzar confided in me and we decided that we should hold a banquet in honour of him, and he would invite all the officials from the other provinces, just to gain their loyalty and acceptance.

"Would you like pigs or bulls?" I asked. A flash of annoyance streaked across his face.

"A hundred of them." He answered bluntly, not answering my question.

"Bulls?" I asked again as he attempted to walk away.

"Sure, it doesn't matter." He answered.

"Would you like wine from here or over there?" I questioned as I pointed to the far off vineyard in the distance..

"This one will do." He quietly tried to slip away, but I knew that in his mind, he would come back because this banquet was just to important to walk out on.

"How many tables shall we bring out?" I thought.

There probably aren't enough spots in the regular dining hall. This time, all the officials, officers, nobles, important people and other invited people will be there. There'll probably have to be over 500 seats. Belshazzar has appointed so many new officials that we might need over 550 seats.

I did the mental arithmetic that if there were already 50 tables, and each table would fit six important people, we would need another 45 tables to make sure that everyone would fit.

"I'll go make sure everything's ready." I spoke to myself as I snapped out of my thoughts. As I entered the rooms, someone was coming over.

"It's almost feast time!" The servant told me.

The sun was almost setting as we watched all the preparations being done.

"Do this!" I shouted to one person to start preparing the wine into goblets.

"Do that!" I shouted to another person to start preparing the bulls to be ready for the table.

"Aren't you going to give us a break?" I heard a person say as I passed by. I ignored him. If they didn't get this done, it would be embarrassment for the King which would mean my head would be separated from my body.

"The wine's ready!" Somebody shouted.

"The bulls are ready!" Another called.

"Okay, set them on the tables." I ordered

"That's good." I said, as the cooks and servants finished the final touches of the feasting tables.

"Have you finished?" The King popped in for a little.

"Yes your majesty." I said.

"Okay, I will bring the people in for the feast." He said. Soon, nobles and officials just kept on streaming into the feasting hall, and all the servants were rushing to and from tables, trying to search for any errors that may have been made.

"You may sit down." The King said. Everybody obeyed.

"Have some wine." King Belshazzar said. We all had a drink from our cups.

"Let the feast begin." He said. All the people rejoiced. The food was great. The wine was good, but however, it wasn't the best I'd ever tasted.

"What's that?" Somebody screamed and out of nowhere, a hand with no visible body appeared, and started printing weird words that I've never heard of. I glanced over at the King. His face was drained of colour. His face was completely white. The letters spelled:

MENE MENE TEKEL UPHARISIN

"What does that mean?" Everyone was asking each other.

"I don't know," The King said, as he called for his wise men to interpret the words. He said that anyone who could interpret the words, would be given the position of Governor, and he would rule all the others, except for the King.

"We don't know." The Wise men said in despair. I knew that all of them wanted to have a high job.

"What shall I do?" The King cried aloud.

"I believe your father had a trusted official who could interpret dreams and signs. His name was Daniel." Belshazzar's mother said as she entered the room.

"Send him to me at once!" Belshazzar ordered a few of his men went out immediately.

"Here I am." Daniel said.

"If you can interpret this dream, I will give you gifts of gold, silver, purple robes you will be clothed in, and you will have a gold chain hanging around your neck- he motioned to me to grab them.

"Keep, your gifts, but I will tell you what the writing means." Daniel said. That's odd. Almost everybody wants gifts from the King. It is like an honour.

"Here's what they mean: Mene means God has numbered the

days of your reign and has brought it to an end. Tekel means you have been weighed on the balances and have not measured up. Parsin your kingdom will be divided and given to the Medes and Persians."

I gasped at the words and didn't believe them.

However, that same night, the Medes and the Persians made their way into Babylon and killed our King! Now I know that Daniel was right. I will never question him about his God again, for I know he is all powerful.

Daniel 5: 1-31

Habakkuk, a Prophet
Interview

Habakkuk was an important prophet in the Old Testament. He prophesied about the Babylonians and warned Judah for their evil acts.

Q: Habakkuk, Can you tell me how the Lord called you?

A: What happened was, the Lord called me to tell the people of Israel about an upcoming Chaldean Invasion if they didn't turn back to him.

Q: Where is Chaldea or who are the Chaldeans?

A: The Chaldeans are also known as the Babylonians. They lived in the Euphrates River Valley and were one of the fiercest fighting tribes in the world.

Q: Ok. So what happened after the Lord called you and told you to prophecy to Israel?

A: Well, first of all I complained.

Q: What did you complain about?

A: Well, I complained about lots of things. I asked the Lord why he was delaying judgement on the Judeans. There was wickedness all around. Looters, Thieves, Deceivers, and many more unrighteous men were in Judah.

Q: Okay, and what was the Lord's answer?

A: The Lord said that Babylonia would conquer Israel when the time was right. He described that their horses were as fast as lightning and that they were ruthless and no nation could stand up against them until the Lord told them the time was right.

Q: How could such a nation be able to conquer nations this quickly?

A: Well, God was on their side, so anything is possible.

Q: Okay, then what happened?

A: Well, I asked God something that really bothered my mind.

Q: What was it?

A: Well, It was why God was using a nation more wicked than Judah to conquer Judah.

Q: So, what answer did the Lord give you?

A: Well, I had to wait for a while before he gave me a clear answer and meaning.

Q: Okay, so what did the Lord say?

A: At first, he didn't give me a clear answer on what he was saying.

Q: What did he say?

A: He said that he would write on the tablet.

Q: I don't seem to get it either.

A: Well, it meant that he was writing the vision right now.

Q: Oh, I see.

A: Yes.

Q: What happened after that?

A: So, God suddenly burst me with a few visions at the same time.

Q: Oh okay. Can you tell me a few?

A: So, the first one was that the Lord was basically saying that he knew how to deal with the proud;.

Q: I don't understand how that has anything to do with the Babylonians.

A: Well, the Babylonians were a proud nation. They were proud of all their achievements and everything.

Q: Ok, I see. I still don't have the meaning entirely yet.

A: Well, the Lord basically said that he knows how to deal with nations that plunder others like Babylon. An example is like Assyria. The Assyrians were the most powerful until they were taken over by the Babylonians.

Q: Oh, I have your point now.

A: Ok, we can move on.

Q: Can you tell me another one of your visions first, though?

A: If you want to.

Q: Okay, let's start.

A: Well, they were all about the same thing. They were saying about how to be careful if you are an idolater, a drunk or greedy person.

Q: First of all, what is an Idolater?

A: It's someone who worships or makes idols.

Q: Well, so how does that have anything to do with Babylon?

A: Well, the Lord said that Babylon was filled with the proud army, Idols, worshipped by the King and the people, and drunks and greedy people.

Q: I still don't get the point.

A: Well, the Lord was saying that Babylon was filled with those, and he knew how to deal with all of those.

Q: Ok, now it seems to make more sense.

A: Well, now it seems like we can move on.

Q: Ok, so is there something you could tell me?

A: Well, the Lord told me that he was all powerful and that he could destroy any nation that was like Babylon.

Q: What did you think of the Lord after that?

A: Well, my whole body trembled, and I bowed down.

Q: Oh, Ok I see. Is there anything else that is important?

A: No, I don't think so.

Q: So God helped you through all that? That's amazing!

A: I know. Praise the Lord!

Habakkuk 1-3

Malachi, the Last Prophet
Interview

Malachi, the last book in the Old Testament was a prophet that prophesied about many things; including the end of the earth.

Q: Malachi, how were you called by the Lord?

A: I was named something before, but the Lord changed my name to Malachi.

Q: Why did he change your name?

A: Well, because Malachi means 'My Messenger.'

Q: What was your old name?

A: I have forgotten my original name, since I have worked for the Lord for so long with the name Malachi.

Q: Why did he name you that?

A: The Lord named me that because I was to prophecy to the Lord's people about what the Lord says.

Q: What kind of things did you prophecy?

A: I prophesied things like how people shouldn't turn away from God and how some people try to cheat God in different ways, but the Lord is the greatest King, and he should be treated like he is.

Q: That's an interesting fact, now, what did you mean by different ways?

A: Some people, they try to cheat God by giving the Lord a crippled or diseased animal for a sacrifice to the Lord, but that cheats the Lord.

Q: Okay, so what did you exactly mean by the sacrifice thing? People had to sacrifice in ancient times had to sacrifice their animals?

A: Not just only animals. They had to sacrifice the purest, non-diseased, smallest, most innocent lamb, to make up for their sins.

Q: Okay, I kind of get your point. Now, why did you have to do all that? Couldn't you just sacrifice something else?

A: No. You had to sacrifice it, because the Lord is all pure and innocent. In order to be with the Lord when we die, we have to be pure and be like him too.

Q: How exactly can sacrificing a lamb help with your life being pure?

A: Well, when the lamb dies, it will take your sin.

Q: Now I see. Didn't you say prophecies? Can you tell me about another prophecy?

A: Well, there was one about people robbing God.

Q: How does that work at all?

A: First, all the people promise to the Lord that they will be faithful, and will give tithes and offerings, but they don't give it, and so they are robbing God.

Q: Okay, I still kind of don't get it though.

A: Well, The Israelites promised the Lord in the desert of Sinai, that they would give the Lord one tenth of what they grew every year as a tithe, and would offer as much as they could to the Lord as offerings. When they don't give it, the priests, who usually get to eat the tithes, go hungry for months.

Q: Thinking about being hungry is making me hungry!

A: Do you want to hear another prophecy?

Q: Ok, if you say so.

A: First of all, the Lord talks about his strength, and then, he is telling me to tell the Judeans that the Day of the Lord is coming.

Q: Whoa, wait a second. What exactly is the day of the Lord?

A: Some people call it the Day of Judgement, some people call it the End of the World, and still others call it The Battle of Evil and Good.

Q: Oh, Ok, so keep on going.

A: Well, he told me to tell them that he would set all the evildoers on fire, and there would not be a branch left on them.

Q: Wait, I don't get that.

A: He meant that he was going to destroy all the evildoers, and not one of them would be left on the earth on that day.

Q: Oh, I think that's a little cruel, but just keep on going.

A: It's not cruel at all. They Lord gave them a fair chance, and they turned it down, they deserve what they get.

Q: Well, if the Lord says so, it's true.

A: The Lord also talks about what happens to his followers.

Q: What happens?

A: He told me that we would be like cattle, and we would trample the wicked and deceit.

Q: I think I get that, now that you've explained the other one.

A: The Lord meant that we would overpower the wicked and all the wicked would be destroyed.

Q: That was just what I was thinking!

A: Well, so then, the Lord told me to tell them to remember the laws of Moses.

Q: Oh and anything else?

A: He also told us that he would strike the earth with a curse on that dreadful day, because it was so horrible.

Q: I wonder how it would be like.

A: I don't think you want to wonder what it's like. It must be like whole battlefield and another few ones all put together.

A: Thank you. What a dreadful prophecy. I'm surprised that Israel and Judah didn't turn back to God immediately.

Malachi 1-4

ACKNOWLEDGEMENTS

First of all, I'd like to thank the Lord, who gives me special interests in reading bible and thinking over. Also, my thanks go to my parents who have always encouraged and prayed for me while I was writing those serial books. I am also indebted to my sisters, who help me challenge some details and edit a lot of parts.

ABOUT THE AUTHOR

Jeremy Jingwei was an eleven-year-old fifth grader when he finished the title. He loves reading and writing. So far he has been author of five titles: *Hundreds of Perspectives Vol One, Frozen Smoke, Blind Shots, Shadows in the Dark, Fallen Behind*, published in the KidPub Press and H2H Books Canada. He currently lives with his parents and his sisters in Barrie, Ontario.

www.ingramcontent.com/pod-product-compliance
Lightning Source LLC
La Vergne TN
LVHW051348080426
835509LV00020BA/3345